The Belhurst Story

David Johnston
9/29/03

The Belhurst Story

David J. Sakmyster

iUniverse, Inc.
New York Lincoln Shanghai

The Belhurst Story

iUniverse, Inc.

For information address:
iUniverse, Inc.
2021 Pine Lake Road, Suite 100
Lincoln, NE 68512
www.iuniverse.com

Cover Photo courtesy of Neil Sjoblom Photography, Geneva, NY

ISBN: 0-595-29369-7

Printed in the United States of America

For Dr. George Maxwell Blackstock Hawley (1870–1941)—engineer, lawyer, teacher and extraordinary historian, without whose tireless researches into the past, without his love for Geneva, and his meticulous notes (fortunately preserved in the Hobart and William Smith College Archives), very little of this story would have been saved.

And a special dedication to Margaret R. Wilson (1920–)—who lived at the Belhurst Castle in her youth while her father served as groundskeeper and chauffeur. She is a historical treasure, and without her memories and stories this tale would have been poignantly incomplete. In her own words, Belhurst will always be her true home. In many ways, this story is for her.

Contents

Acknowledgments

A great many people aided in the realization of this work, and if I leave anyone out it is with the sincere apologies of one who may have lost count of how much help he has received.

First, my gratitude goes out to Karen Osborne at the Geneva Historical Society, who helped set my feet onto this path, and who kindly dealt with every one of my "just one last thing…" requests. To Linda Benedict at the Warren Hunting Smith Library Archives, Hobart and William Smith Colleges. To Dale Johnson from the New York State Folklore Society and to the Ontario County Records Archives.

To my Uncle Thomas Sakmyster from the University of Cincinnati, and Linda Bailey at the Cincinnati, Ohio Historical Society—both pulling through with some key records when I needed them most.

I would also like to thank the *Finger Lakes Times* for their record-keeping skills and excellent journalism throughout most of Geneva's history. Also to Maud Kane at the Yates County Office of Public History, who found a critical missing piece of the puzzle, and to the Oliver House Historical Museum in Penn Yan.

A special thanks also goes to Carmen Brennan, Banquet Manager at Belhurst Castle, and to several members of the current staff; also I am indebted to Dr. Kamil Kovach, "Red" Dwyer's physician towards the end of his life.

For their invaluable databases and meticulous genealogical collections, I thank the Family History Center (at The Church of Jesus Christ of Latter Day Saints) in Pittsford, NY.

To Margaret Wilson, who kept not only those amazing photographs of the Collins' era, but also kept alive such incredible memories and stories of her youth.

And finally, my thanks goes to my wife, Amy, who has given invaluable editorial assistance, helped with the research, encouraged me when I faltered, and endured my moods throughout this obsession.

Foreword

"Oh, they're stories here. The place is lousy with 'em. It's hard, though, to tell the fiction from the fact." [1]

—Cornelius "Red" Dwyer (Owner and operator of Belhurst Castle
1933-1975)

On the outskirts of Geneva NY, it stands in a beautiful grove amidst ancient oak trees, high on a cliff with a sweeping view of Seneca Lake. It is a castle in a style and grace rarely seen this side of the Atlantic. Constructed with red Medina limestone, its dormers, balconies and turrets stand in stoic repose, as if contemplating a long and memorable past. Inside, the exquisitely carved oak craftsmanship and mahogany fixtures whisper of bygone days of glory; in the foyer a suit of armor patiently stands guard before a winding staircase while above, eleven elegant guest rooms jealously retain over a century of secrets.

In the winter of 2000, as a birthday gift I surprised my soon-to-be wife Amy by taking her to the Belhurst Castle where we would stay a night on the top floor—in the Tower Suite, overlooking the grounds and the lake. After a spirited evening socializing with local patrons in the mahogany-walled tavern on the first floor, under an approving smile from a large gold-framed painting of the late owner, Cornelius Dwyer, we retired to the widow's peak in our room for a sip of champagne.

Looking out over the dark front lawn, snow-free during an unusual January thaw, we gazed silently at the moon-speckled lake, and then suddenly—we froze. Something on the lawn just below us caught our attention at the same moment. My wife recollects that she took her eyes away from the figure only to see the hairs on my neck standing on end.

I was riveted to the sight—there, standing between two large evergreen bushes, staring out over the lake, was a woman dressed in a magnificent white gown. My heart raced as my eyes struggled to make sense of the image, to place it as perhaps some trick of the moon playing off the hedges, or the interior dining room lights casting odd reflections. But the more we looked, the clearer she

---

1. "The Redhead Squire of Belhurst", Rochester D&C Interview, August 9, 1970.

became, and there, at two in the morning on a Friday evening, I wrestled with something I couldn't comprehend.

We watched, just staring in silence for another five minutes at the motionless figure that solemnly faced eastward. At that point I wanted to run down the three flights of stairs and race onto the lawn to see her up close, even though I was sure she would be gone when I arrived.

Amy, however, pulled me away from the window, whispering that whoever it was, and she had no doubt it was a ghost, "didn't want to be seen." We were intruding on her privacy, perhaps on some melancholy ritual she performed in the darkest hours or under the moon's light, a somber experience that wasn't meant for others to see.

Reluctantly, I pulled away. We went to sleep. At least Amy did. I, however, had the worst night's sleep of my life, fitfully drawing close to sleep, then jarred awake by knocking sounds at the windows, scraping in the pipes, scratching at the doors, and what sounded like footsteps on the winding stairs up the turret.

Later, we put the incident out of our heads, and for myself, despite a great interest in the supernatural, including writing about it in fictional tales for years, having never been privileged to actually witness anything so unusual, I wrote off the vision. In time, I thought back on it and almost convinced myself it was a trick of the light—so realistic that at two in the morning it played on our senses and our brains interpreted the image the same way. Or, I thought, maybe she was just an eager bride dressed up and strolling the grounds the night before her wedding. (However, I recently verified through Belhurst's records that they did not host a wedding that weekend.)

The only thing that gave me pause was that in checking out the next morning, as we rounded the final turn in the stairs to the dining room, we stopped to glance at a framed set of old black and white photos on the wall.

There, in an ancient picture, posed in a chair, wearing an intricate white dress, a woman sat with her chin in her hand, looking almost expectantly at me. I marked the caption and noted that her name was Carrie Collins, and it was her vision that built this castle in the late 1880s. Dry-mouthed, I blinked, and continued on my way down the stairs, and thought nothing more of this.

Until that is, one October evening in 2002. Amy, now my wife, was flipping through the channels while we ate dinner (the joys of TV dining), and she stopped on the news where they were featuring a Halloween story on local hauntings. And there flashed a picture of the Belhurst Castle, and the announcer said, very matter-of-factly, that for years people have been seeing a 'Lady in White' on the grounds, and many believe the whole place to be haunted. The story went on to relate a tale about an Opera Singer and a love affair that ended in tragedy, with the singer's ghost remaining behind in romantic desolation.

We both dropped our forks and our jaws.

And from that day until now, in my spare time and any other time I could whittle away, I have picked and chipped at the history of the Belhurst Castle, desperate to understand what we, and apparently many others, have seen. Along the way I've found that the Lady in White is just one of the cornerstones of astounding experiences and events at this setting. I've excavated pieces of the legends, stripping away fiction from fact where possible, and out of necessity and perhaps obsession, I've uncovered far more than I originally set out to understand. Beyond even any supernatural events, there are truths here stranger than fiction.

All the answers are not here, but what is assembled in the following chapters I hope comes close to doing justice not only to the prevailing folklore about the Belhurst Castle, but to the whole history of one of the most intriguing sites in upstate New York. It is a plot of land that has seen more than its share of adventure, romance, passion and tragedy. With some of the most colorful characters of those times, with deep mysteries and deeper superstitions, there are, as Dwyer said, stories here, and many of those will be told in the coming pages.

I can't help but think of old Cornelius Dwyer, in his last days at the Castle, up in the suite where the roulette wheel once spun, doing his own obsessive research into Belhurst's history. And how, thirty years later, I'm walking in his footsteps—although stepping deeper and going farther than he had been able to with the tools at his disposal.

Hopefully the coming chapters will highlight the richness of this enduring landmark, resolve some intriguing mysteries and shed light on its complex history, painting an image of something that seems at times to have a life of its own—or at the very least, a soul. Perhaps, though, it always had one. The Seneca Indians who originally lived on this land had a belief in what they called *Orenda*—a lifeforce ingrained in the sacred landscape; it was an invisible power and a transmissible spiritual energy pervading all things.

I've often thought back on that night three years ago, to that vision on the lawn, when my wife told me to look away. But, with apologies to her, it was a request I couldn't honor, and in the past eight months, I wonder if maybe she was wrong, and that the woman we saw in fact wanted just the opposite: she wanted me to look.

To dig, to search.

I have looked. With excitement and trepidation at times, sadness and exhilaration at others, I have looked.

Here is what I have found.

1

Facts and Early History

"Life is infinitely stranger than anything the mind of man could invent."

—Sherlock Holmes,
<u>The Hound of the Baskervilles</u>

Setting aside the fabulous legends surrounding the Belhurst Castle property, for which there is little validation but as we shall see, some historical reference, we can begin with the facts that are readily ascertained.

The area about Belhurst Castle was originally the site of the Seneca Indian Village of Kanadesaga, home to the Council of the Six Nations of the Iroquois (the first successful 'United Nations'). Historian Robert Conover states that "…it was a village laid out in circular form, with buildings made of bark and hewn logs…many of them were of the rudest style of Indian architecture, indicating the great age of the town."[1]

---

1. E. Thayles Emmons, <u>The Story of Geneva</u>.

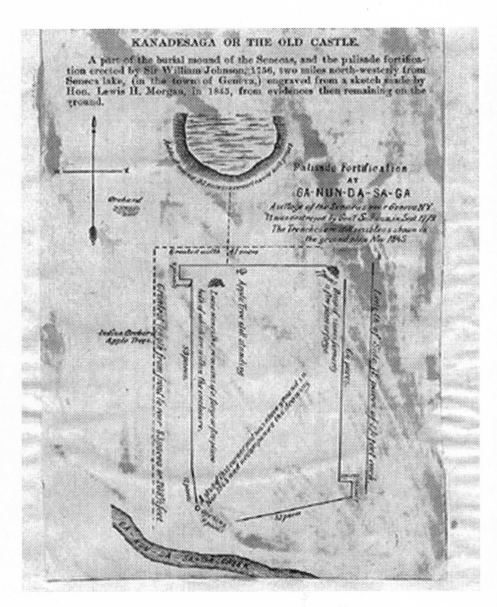

Illustration courtesy of The Geneva Historical Society

In 1756, Sir William Johnson of England helped the Iroquois build stockades and palisades surrounding Kanadesaga as protection against French incursions. Interestingly, because of these palisades, the Indian towns that had them were referred to as 'Castles'. Kanadesaga was termed 'Old Castle' up until the time of its destruction.

Because of Kanadesaga's strategic importance on the outlet of Seneca Lake, the British had a strong presence there, and during the early years of the Revolutionary War, the British at Kanadesaga were led by the Tory, Walter Butler. In May of 1778, he convinced the chief 'sachem', or leader of the Senecas, Old Smoke, that the American Army had designs on their land. They launched a pre-emptive strike which resulted in the infamous massacre of Colonial settlers in Wyoming Valley, PA.

It was this battle which forced General Washington's hand against the 'Indian threat'. He sent a force led by General Sullivan to revenge the Wyoming Massacre and to put a stop to the Indian incursions.

In 1779, after many battles along the way where they depleted the bulk of the Iroquois and Tory forces, General Sullivan's forces reached Kanadesaga and found it empty but for a small starved white boy crying in the midst of the burned fortress (he had been one of the captives from Wyoming Valley). Sullivan and his army were impressed with the beauty of the site, its plush apple orchards and sweeping lake views.

After the Revolutionary War, Britain made no provision for the native tribes of New York State who had been her allies. Many of the newly independent Americans desired vengeance for the great savagery carried out against them during the war, but Washington urged compassion, and with Governor George Clinton of NY, they recognized the Indians as the owners of the soil. Preparations were begun to negotiate with them for the land.

The current Belhurst site was originally part of a 223-acre lot owned by the State of Massachusetts but purchased by land developers Oliver Phelps and Nathaniel Gorham on April 1, 1788. (It was part of a $1 million dollar, six million acre deal—the historic Phelps and Gorham Purchase that took all of the contested Massachusetts land titles from Western NY). As impressive as this purchase was, the more difficult negotiations lay ahead, with the Indian tribes who were growing increasingly uncomfortable with pioneer advancement and distrustful of the new nation's ability to honor post-war treaties.

Phelps and Gorham prevailed, after long negotiations with rivals New York Genesee Land Company and a group of British speculators from Canada known as the Niagara Genesee Land Company. Each of these companies had a stronger relationship with the Indian tribes, and Phelps and Gorham had their work cut out for them. The current settlers, joining behind Jonathan Livingston and the New York Genesee Land Company, were even threatening secession from New

York to protect their claims. Oliver Phelps, finally as a show of faith, offered a portion of his own shares to these current landowners, which won them over. Then, through difficult but ultimately successful debates at a council in Buffalo Creek, he won agreement from the Indians to cede their lands for a small sum of money.

Phelps, in the summer of 1788, was also struck by the beauty of Kanadesaga and remarked that "we mean to found a city here." Soon, the village was formally renamed Geneva and it became the rendezvous of traders going to the Great Lakes. Taverns and cottages sprung up, and surveyors, speculators and explorers arrived, all seized by the fever of hope and ambition. Phelps and Gorham soon sold their unused land portion to Robert Morris in 1790, who in turn sold his title to Sir William Pulteney, John Harnbey and Patrick Colqumann of London.

William Pulteney, reputedly the wealthiest man in Britain, had decided to invest in American Real estate. However, not being American and thus disqualified by the new country's real estate acquisition laws, he needed a loophole. He found one in a man named Charles Williamson.

In 1781 Captain Williamson, a dissatisfied veteran of Britain's twenty-fifth regiment, crossed the Atlantic with letters of introduction to Lord Cornwallis in his luggage. He was met, however, by the U.S. vessel Marquis of Salem, and Williamson was taken prisoner. Since he was a non-combatant, he actually did not go to an American prison, but to the pleasant confines of one Ebenezer Newell's home in Roxbury, Massachusetts. During his confinement he apparently made an impression; by the time he returned to England he had married young Abigail Newell. Back in England, Williamson's father had formed close connections with Pulteney, and it was this association, along with Charles's experience during the intervening years in politics and agricultural experimentation, and his extensive knowledge of American rules and attitudes, that brought him into Pulteney's favor.

He sent Williamson to America, where his wife was only too glad to return, and he became naturalized in 1792; he walked out of the courtroom a proprietor of one of the largest pieces of property in the world.

He traveled his new lands extensively, providing tireless efforts to settle and expand the American frontiers. It was upon his first visit to the settlement by Seneca Lake that he used the name "Geneva", describing the favorable hospitality he received there, and remarking to find so large a body of water as this lake still free from ice at that time of year. However, as historian Dr. George Hawley relates, it was not Williamson (as tradition held for some time) that named the town Geneva due to a resemblance to its European counterpart. In actuality, letters by fur traders in the area show that the name had already been in use for several years previously.

Williamson was constantly on the move, exploring and developing settlements on the Pulteney lands; eventually he set his family up in Bath, NY as his permanent residence, although as we are to see, he kept another home in Geneva. A 300-acre lot owned by Williamson was called 'Two Mile Point Farm', and extended along the lake and included "some of the most interesting historical places and events to be chronicled."[2] He was a great believer in the adage that nothing succeeds like excess, and between 1794 and 1797 he built a palatial house on the property, at the south termination of the street on a summit of ground running along the west side of the lake, having an unobstructed view of the entire street. Records show it cost $9,577 to build—at that time an enormous sum—and it must have stood in stark grandeur compared to the surrounding rudimentary barns and log cabins.[3]

When the investments didn't pan out as Pulteney planned (at least not in the timeframe and scope he had anticipated), funding dried up. Williamson returned to Scotland around 1800; he died there in 1808. His successor, agent William P. Dana, and his family lived in Williamson's Geneva house until 1804 when his wife died and he returned to England. The house, as we shall see in the next chapters, was soon afterwards destroyed in a fire.

In 1810, 223 acres (of Williamson's 300 total) were sold for $3,000 to the Ontario Glass Manufacturing Company, which became incorporated in that year. In 1822 the Glass Company separated the 200 acres north of the factory and divided it among eleven stockholders. The 23 acres to the south consisted of the factory itself plus a colony of tenant houses for workmen on the West side of the road.

The primary stockholder, receiving 35 acres, was one William DeZeng, and as such, he received the most desirable acreage. DeZeng was the son of a Saxon nobleman who, among other enterprises, was involved in the early improvements of waterways in NY. William Steuben DeZeng was named in honor of Baron Steuben who was, at the time of DeZeng's birth, making one of his periodic visits to his friend, Major DeZeng. The Baron, a bachelor and pleased that his namesake was being used, remembered it by leaving young William a thousand acres of land.[4] For half a century, DeZeng was identified with the growth and develop-

---

2.   G.M.B. Hawley, "Chronicles of Geneva", *The Geneva Daily Times*, May 21, 1921.
3.   Ibid.
4.   E. Thayles Emmons, "The Story of Geneva

ment of the town and the surrounding areas, and especially with the development of the Glassworks, eventually buying out the company. He also was involved with the creation of Hobart College and was one of the originators of the Manhattan Life Insurance Company, which he founded during one of many frequent trips to New York City.

His deed on May 5, 1824 recites that the lot on this property included a house, a barn and a well, all located on the hill near the road, about 300 feet to the north.[5] A factory superintendent named DeWitt probably occupied the house, being a short distance from the workmen's tenant homes. In 1827 DeZeng sold his land for $911 to the Reverend Orin Clark of Geneva, who already owned 56 acres of land on the property directly opposite this site.

Reverend Clark died only a year later. He had been the first official minister of Trinity Presbyterian Episcopal Church in 1813, and he was influential in transferring the old Geneva Academy into Geneva College, now part of Hobart and William Smith Colleges.

Clark's executors sold his 91 acres to Joseph Fellows for $2,706 on Sept. 4, 1833. Fellows, one of the initial stockholders of the Ontario Glass Company (who started with 26 shares), had been buying up all the other lots, and by this time had acquired them all except for the Glass Factory site on the south side (the location of the current Geneva Country Club).

Fellows was a native of Warwickshire, England, and came to America in 1795 with his father. He had settled in Pennsylvania and became a lawyer. In 1810, as an agent of the Pulteney Land Office, he was sent to Geneva to oversee their operations, taking over after the death of Colonel Troup. (Troup, as William P. Dana's successor, had been residing in Williamson's mansion for a time).

The "History of the Pioneer Settlement", published in 1851, describes Fellows as "an agent who managed business with strict integrity and in the same spirit of liberality and indulgence that actuated his predecessor."[6]

Between the years of 1830 and 1835 one of the most curious events in Geneva history would occur, one that will be fully explored in Chapter Three. Fellows actually owned the land purchased from DeZeng under a deed of trust for a mysterious gentleman named Henry Hall. Hall had recently arrived from England and he oddly refused to have any property in his own name; instead, he had Fellows hold the deed and all his considerable funds on behalf of a striking woman he had brought with him from overseas.

---

5.   G.M.B. Hawley, "Chronicles of Geneva," *Geneva Daily Times*, May 28, 1921.
6.   Turner, "History of the Pioneer Settlement", 1851.

For four years, Hall lived in a small house previously owned by the Glassworks superintendent, with this woman and his son. In early 1835, they moved into a newly completed English-style mansion on the same property. He called this new home that he had built 'The Hermitage'; however, he died that summer and had little time to enjoy it.[7]

It was this mansion, the Hermitage, with its gabled roofs and angled porches, that for many years would exert a great mystique among the townspeople, ultimately leading to hushed tales about an underground tunnel and stashed wealth. The whispers that had surfaced earlier during the time of the reclusive and mysterious Henry Hall only grew more and more urgent and took on a life of their own, especially later, when this home was left vacant for years.

After Hall's death, the woman quickly sold the property back to Fellows, who in turn sold it to two brothers, James C. and Daniel B. Brown on March 18, 1836 for $10,862. They actually received this lot plus the others owned by Fellows—almost 200 acres.[8]

In 1852, Augustus Brown, likely a son of James and Margaret Brown, sold 51.5 acres to Robert H. Boyd for $7,500. Boyd held the property for only a few months, selling it on November 17, 1852 to "General" Harrison G. Otis. The Otis family named the scenic grove on the property Bellehurst, which meant "beautiful forest". The site changed ownership many times within the Otis family (Harrison and Mary, and their relatives William and Ann Otis and their children all stayed there at some point), and soon the newspapers began calling the area the 'Otis Place'.

It was rumored that during the Civil War, the area was used as a stop on the Underground Railroad, and that a hidden tunnel served as a hiding place for runaway slaves on their trek to Canada.

On March 27, 1878 the United States Trust Company of New York acquired the title from Mary Otis for $15,208.[9] The Otis's moved to Virginia, and their reason for leaving Geneva may have had something to do with a loss of other land rights through reassessment to Glenwood Cemetery.

The United States Trust Company held the land (and the unoccupied mansion) from 1878 until November 29, 1884 when it was transferred to Susan Bergan (a portion of the land was sold off to Henry Slosson). During this time it had been a popular picnic site for townspeople and a spot for young lovers, and was

---

7. G.M.B. Hawley, Scrapbook of Geneva Homes, William Hunting Smith Archives, Hobart College, 1936.
8. Abstract of Land Title, Geneva NY.
9. Ibid.

referred to as 'Otis Grove'. The legends spread, as did the rumors of the haunted house. It remained unoccupied, and young children and teenagers frequently explored the grounds and the dilapidated mansion, looking for spooks and hidden tunnels that reportedly wound down to the lake.

The mansion, with its large leaded glass bay windows, some of them broken, others caked over with dirt, probably gave the appearance of mystery, which only fueled the scary stories.

Susan Bergan, strangely, sold the property within only a month. It is unclear if she ever moved into the house—or perhaps she did and then decided for some reason to move right out. On Dec 24, 1884 she transferred the house and property back to the United States Trust Company.

In 1885 there arrived in Geneva a wealthy woman from New York City. She came with her manager, having heard stories about the beauty of this grove. Immediately she fell in love with the site, asked the purchase price, and paid the $12,000 on the spot.

Her name was Carrie Harron, and her story too will be told in greater detail in a later chapter. For now, it is enough to know that within a year she divorced her husband and married her companion, Captain Louis Dell Collins, and together they set out on a three-year construction project creating what was to become the Belhurst Castle in place of the old Hermitage.

After Carrie's death in 1926, her grandson Hal Harron Jr. inherited the Castle and the grounds. Immersed suddenly in vast wealth, young Hal left Geneva almost immediately, moved to Bermuda and traveled extensively. He leased the Castle first to a family named Parmalee from Canada—but they too, like Susan Bergan, moved out quickly. In two months they were gone, claiming they couldn't stay there since it was haunted.[10]

In 1932, a young Irishman from nearby Lyons, NY became interested in the Castle. Cornelius J. Dwyer was nearly broke, but looking to recapture a life of luxury and class he had lost with the stock market crash. Dwyer leased the land and the Belhurst Castle until 1946, when he bought it outright. During this time, under Dwyer's extensive vision and skillful management, the Belhurst Castle became one of the finest dining establishments on the East Coast, and was at times, a speakeasy, casino and a supper club. Its fame soared and it attracted people from across the country.

---

10.   Interview with Margaret Wilson, August 2003.

In 1975, the aging Dwyer sold Belhurst Castle and its grounds to Robert J. Golden, who maintained it until 1992 when the current owner, Duane R. Reeder took over.

Each of these eras has its own unique story, and is intriguing in many ways, and most of these tales will be explored in more detail.

But first...having brushed over the factual timeline and introduced the major characters, we can turn to the myths. The legends that exist today were ones that grew from the mysteries of the early 1800s, when Geneva was growing and finding its identity, when grand events were sweeping across the fledgling nation, when superstitions ran high, and tales of romance and adventure were hungrily sought after.

There are many astounding tales about the Belhurst site, stretching back to the days of the native Indians, but one story in particular has held fast to the minds and hearts of many Genevans...

2

Legends

"History is the version of past events that people have decided to agree upon."

—Napoleon Bonaparte (1769-1821)

It is the most romantic of the legends that stir the imagination of those who know and love Belhurst Castle. Any Web search on the Belhurst Castle and the word "haunted" will mention it. The tale has been printed in a recent issue of Reader's Digest, commented on in television shows, and invoked in many articles throughout the years.

However, as folklore goes, it is one of the more difficult tales to unravel and is decidedly confounding to determine its origins. All we have is the story written by noted scholar and folktale expert, Carl Carmer, in his 1936 book chronicling early New York folktales, Listen for a Lonesome Drum. Unfortunately, Carmer does not reference his sources for these numerous short legends, and he has long since passed away.

There are however, elements to this tale that can be traced to fact, as we shall discover later. But here, now, I will relate the legend, taking just a few narrative liberties with Carmer's tale:

The Opera Singer and the Spanish Don

Before there was the Belhurst Castle, before Otis Grove existed and before even the town was developed, a gray stone house sat on a cliff overlooking the beautiful Seneca Lake. A Spanish gentleman with dark, flowing hair and a thick mustache curling over smiling lips held a blond woman's hand as they sat and enjoyed the view. She squinted from the blazing sun reflecting off the rippling lake beneath them, and she squeezed his hand tightly, as if separation would mean her end. Her white dress rippled slowly in a light breeze that meandered over the cliff and whistled through the eaves of great oak branches.

"Do you think they'll find us?" she asked, even though she knew it angered him. It was a question she voiced often during these past two years, ever since they had finished the home with the help of the Natives, and had since lived in peaceful solitude.

"Do not think on it," he said. "We are prepared."

She nodded and sighed, closing her eyes and basking in the warmth of the sun. The first winter, when they had just arrived, had been difficult; and the last one even colder, but it had given them time to prepare for the worst, and surely it slowed down their pursuers.

"The tunnel..." she whispered.

"Is complete. The passage descends slightly, but is straight until the stairs, then angles downward sharply to the shore where our boat awaits. And the trap is rigged—one pull of the lever and it will collapse behind us." He turned and gently stroked her cheek. "But they will not find us, they're not that good."

"Yes they are," she responded. "And they are paid by a rich woman scorned."

"Do not remind me of my wife."

"Why not? It's true. You left her for me—"

"For love."

"And killed my suitor."

"Again, for love."

"I know."

"For love. And for your voice."

She took a deep breath. "Which will never again grace the opera halls, or rise in honor of the unrivaled Italian composers."

"Better to be silenced than to have me suffer in jealousy while the whole world basks in your beauty."

A soft smile came to her lips. "My Don, what have we done?"

"Only what we must," he replied.

And together they sat and sipped dark red wine while the sun descended and the oak trees cast reaching shadows toward them.

The dogs were barking before dawn. The Don awoke with a start, sliding out from under his mistress's arm. He peered out the window and saw the flickering torchlights bobbing up and down, men approaching on horseback from west and north.

His heart sank. "Too soon," he cried as he turned and lifted the woman in her long ivory nightgown from the bed. "It's time," he whispered as he carried her to the trap door.

She awoke fully on the way down and carried the torch ahead as they raced through the soft earthen tunnel carved out only months before. They had to stoop, and in minutes her dress was covered with twigs, dirt and mud. Stopping only once to con-firm their fears, they pressed on as soon as the shouts and footfalls of the Spaniards were heard behind them, gaining.

"Not much farther to the stairs," he said, pulling his lover by the hand. "Almost there, almost to the switch! Our gold is in boxes below, and our boat is just beyond. We're free."

A tiny smile crept across his face, unnoticed by the woman as she pulled free from him and bent to retrieve the torch she had dropped.

"Leave it," he cried as he pressed on, shouting to make his voice heard over the trampling of approaching feet. Come on, *he thought giddily,* all of you rush forward into the tunnel. Just a little further and there will be no one to chase us on the lake.

He reached the stairwell and there, in the flickering torchlight, the wooden lever poised skyward, expectantly. "Now, my love," he whispered without looking back, "down the stairs!"

Something rushed by him—a light presence or a faint touch—but it was enough. She was safe, he thought, and he threw the switch. Racing down the stairs after her, excitement coursing in his veins, he burst through the cloud of swirling dust and dirt from the collapsing tunnel, his footsteps clapping over the muffled cries of suffocating Spaniards, and he rushed out the bottom exit and onto the lakeshore.

Where he stood in the glorious pre-dawn starlight.

Alone.

He blinked and breathlessly turned around and around. The boat stood anchored, quietly rising and falling with a somber tide while a cool breeze blew away the dust from his eyes, only to chill the newly forming tears.

He stared at the open passageway and the darkness leading back up to the tunnel. He stared and waited, and waited.

Dawn came slowly and reluctantly, as if fearing the Don's wrath when light would not bring relief.

Hours later, the lone figure set off on the small boat. There were no provisions, and he carried with him none of the treasure from the tunnels.

He had lost something far more valuable.

He sailed into the rising sun, and while the rest of his days were spent back in Europe in silent contemplation at a Roman monastery, in his mind he really never left that shore on Seneca Lake.

And to this day, neither has the Opera Singer, who walks the grounds in desola-tion, grieving for her lost love and the tragedy of their fate.

◆　　◆　　◆

This story's first appearance, as far as records go, is with Carmer's tale, although one would think it must have been in the oral tradition years before. However, as I will show in the next chapter, Geneva was blessed with three very thorough and professional historians who chronicled in great detail the town's early history. The fact that this tale, such a tragic and memorable drama which positively cries out for verification, was not only ignored but not even mentioned in any way before 1936 is very interesting, and lends itself to a fascinating critical study of myth creation. As it stands today, all the literature and traditions hold that the vision of the Lady in White at the Belhurst Castle is this Opera Singer of myth.

But we will let that story sit for now. Since it took me almost a year to unravel its origins, we can wait another chapter before revealing the truth.

Burial Mounds

As if this story was not enough to regale visitors and provide the local Genevans with their own enduring romantic legend, something about this site seems to draw out other fantastic tales.

Maybe the origin of so many rumors and legends about this area is simply a byproduct of the wealthy characters that have decided to build their palatial homes here—and the natural mistrust that created—or maybe it is something more.

From the earliest times, even before the village of Kanadesaga was formed, this section of land held an aura of mystery. The Finger Lakes themselves were places of great power to the Indians—they believed the lakes were formed when the great god set his hand in the earth, pressing firmly until the seas spread into the depressions left by his fingers. The Seneca origin myth maintains that their people emerged from a hole in the Great Hill, but a huge serpent ate them all, except for a boy and girl. They shot the serpent, which promptly released all the bones of their relatives, which are now in a mound at the bottom of the lake.

The belief in burial mounds is an important one to Kanadesaga, as the Six Nations had at their capital here their most sacred burial mound. To the Senecas, veneration of the dead was a defining trait, and the graves of their ancestors were the dearest spots on earth; they were ever ready to defend them to the death. As part of the land cession to Phelps and Gorham, the Indians insisted that the white man promise to respect that mound and never disturb its contents. It sounds like an overdone horror theme, but "there is a tradition among the old residents of Geneva that [the Indians] swore eternal vengeance against the hand that should disturb the bones in the Old Castle mound."[1]

Interestingly, the historian George Conover, in his 1879 tour of the lands, did just that—the first white man to excavate there, although only slightly. He confirmed that there was a human skeleton at a depth of two feet, along with several articles that the Indians bury with their dead. A few of these pieces (a copper kettle, some pipe bowls, cloth and a belt buckle) were given to the Waterloo Historical Society, except for one of the pipe bowls which Conover kept for himself. "The same afternoon several parties discovered other skeletons and the top of a skull of a child ten or twelve years old was unearthed."[2] The mound is about forty feet in diameter and four feet high.

For many years after 1780, Native Americans continued to visit the spot annually to ensure that the mound was preserved; these visitors grew less and less in number as the years passed. Finally, their pilgrimages ceased altogether. The white man stuck to his promise, but while the site was not disturbed, nor was it much honored. A small headstone marks its spot in a field behind a gas station and an old garage, just past the intersection of Pre-emption and Old Castle Roads.

---

1.   E. Thayles Emmons, <u>The Story of Geneva</u>.
2.   Ibid., p. 103.

Other burial mounds dotted the area, and it is not known if they fared much better. There is an interesting story of one mound, six feet in diameter, not far from the old Fort, where tradition holds that a powerful giant was slain and his great bones covered with earth. The Senecas used this spot as a sacred place to continue burying their relatives. Historian and writer E. Thayles Emmons thought it would be interesting to excavate this mound and see if such a giant existed, but nothing was done that he knew about.

However, a story in the *Geneva Gazette* in 1888 notes that the Rev. J.W. Sanborn, an authority on the history of the Seneca Indians, had been prospecting in Ontario County for the buried remains of Indians. He was "rewarded while excavating in an old burying ground on the farm of Mr. Squires in Gorham, exhuming quite complete skeletons of two males and one female, at least 150 years in the ground."[3] One of the bodies apparently was thought to be the largest Indian skull ever found in America, with a femur of nineteen inches in length, indicating he had to have been over seven and half feet tall. Additionally, he had been wounded on the upper back part of the head. This skeleton went to Cambridge, England for further study, the results of which are not known.

A final tradition among the Indians is that of a great Council Tree where the tribes would hold rituals and make important decisions, as well as bury their dead. This tree stood until 1930.

The relevance of burials on this land continued with the early settlers. Emmons relates that the season of 1795 in particular was very sickly, and there were many deaths in Geneva. As of this time however, there was no cemetery. "In early days it was quite common to set apart a place on the farm for family burial purposes..."[4]

So all this is to point out that in addition to who may or may not be in mysterious collapsed tunnels, there were evidently a great many bodies under the earth here long before the advent of the Pulteney Burial Ground and later cemeteries. Many of the bodies were later re-interred, but not all of them could be found, as tombstones were costly and scarcely used.

---

3. *Geneva Gazette*, June 8, 1888.
4. Ibid., p. 115

Haunted Houses

If there is any basis for beliefs that the dead remain to haunt the living, then there are ample candidates for populating the three so-called Haunted Houses which existed on the current Belhurst property through the years.

The first house to earn that reputation was Captain Williamson's mansion on Two-Mile Point Farm. Construction on the house finished after several years in 1797 and was occupied by Williamson during his periodic visits and sojourns in Geneva. Other residents of the house included fellow Pulteney Land Officers William Pulteney Dana, Colonel Robert Troup and General George Goundry. Troup was one of the early benefactors of community development in Geneva and an honored Trustee of Hobart College from 1833 to 1873. He had even tried to give the house and some of the land to Hobart College, but the grant was not accepted. He lived in the house until the legal affairs of the land office were given to Joseph Fellows who, as we read before, was one of the stockholders in the Ontario Glass Company.[5]

Fellows did not stay in the house; the mansion fell into disrepair and became dilapidated. Historian George Hawley states that in his research he could not find references as to the disposition of the house, but tradition held that it had later been destroyed by fire. There are also stories that Captain Williamson's son, building a new home across town for his young bride, utilized portions from this house in its construction.

"No doubt the remainder was removed or destroyed by fire for it must have been an unsightly ruin and...an unwelcome reminder of the former greatness of his father."[6] In any case, the unoccupied house and its later ruin became known to the early Genevans as "The Haunted House", a title this residence would retain until another took its place a half century later.

When Joseph Fellows sold his lands to the Browns, Daniel and James, a new mansion, the Hermitage, had just been completed, and the first home of Henry Hall (the former DeWitt home), 200 feet to the west, was converted into a barn. The Browns stayed in the mansion until 1852 when the Otis family took it over. By the time Carrie Harron purchased the property in 1885 and fixed up the home, "the stories of the 'Haunted House' were many. That is not so long ago but that many citizens of Geneva recall the old dilapidated house with its strange towers and gables."[7] Hawley himself remembers his days as a youth spent at the

---

5.   G.M.B. Hawley, "Chronicles of Geneva," *Geneva Daily Times*, May 21, 1921.

6.   G.M.B. Hawley, "Chronicles of Geneva," *Geneva Daily Times*, May 21, 1921.

7.   Ibid., May 28, 1921.

site, exploring the ruins of the eerie palatial home. "The windows were mostly destroyed and the doors gone, so that the curious youth, and often adults, searched the house from top to bottom in vain hope of meeting Mr. or Mrs. Spook."[8]

Photographs courtesy of The Geneva Historical Society

8.   Ibid.

Here we have the first hint of a possible connection to the Carmer folktale—as it was this house which was rumored to have a secret underground passage to Seneca Lake through the large staircase at the end of the main hall. Hawley dispels this myth, however, and relates how the tunnel story likely arose from the existence of a safe deposit vault under the dining room which was accessed through a movable panel. He says that he and another youth, Horace Webster, were among those who regularly visited the site looking for tunnels and treasures. All they found was a small blind cellar, about two-thirds filled with earth, which at first, could not be explained.

He goes on to say that Mr. Louis Collins later told him that during the excavation for the Belhurst Castle's new foundation, the secret cellar was discovered and "it was found to be like a vault without exit or entrance anywhere, a solid wall having been built by a later owner of the house across the panel entrance."[9] Collins also told him he found a brick from the old foundation with the date "1835" inscribed in it, marking that it was there when the foundation to the cellar was set (with Hall's construction of the Hermitage).

Later, Hawley learned the truth from his aunt. Apparently Mary Otis told Hawley's aunt (in 1860) the story about this panel and the vault, and the fact that her husband had sealed up the vault after swearing the workmen to secrecy. Apparently Mr. Otis had hired a carpenter to do some interior work and while making some repairs to the dining room this carpenter discovered a loose panel. He was suspicious and curious, and removed it only to find a ladder leading down to an empty cellar. Mary Otis told Hawley's aunt that she believed it was this carpenter that later spread rumors of an 'Arabian Nights' theme about the place, having hidden passages all over and possibly more such ladders leading to gold.

"The stories became so prevalent and the visitors arrived so frequently to search for the spooks and secret passage of escape that Mary Otis had the cellar filled with earth and brick without acknowledging its existence, thus avoiding publicity and description of the place. She replaced the moveable panel with a solid wall"[10] and commanded the workmen and Hawley's aunt to secrecy "so that the story would not be told during her lifetime lest the acknowledgment, added to the mystery of (Henry) Hall, might prejudice the sale of the house or cause her annoyance."[11]

9.   *The Geneva Daily Times*, "History of Belhurst Castle", Nov. 11, 1959.
10.   *Geneva Daily Times*, May 28, 1921.
11.   Ibid.

Hawley obviously took great delight in this discovery and felt it finally put to rest theories of underground passages and rumored treasure. It is fascinating however, that no one conclusively stated who built the cellar. Hawley in one document states that General Otis built it for use as a safe deposit vault for those frequent times he was called away on military duty (there were no safe deposit boxes in Geneva yet). In another (earlier) article, he says Mrs. Otis claims the Browns built it for use as a vault, although more out of fear since in the wooded grove with no neighbors they were isolated and vulnerable. All the other rumors of course, were that the wealthy Henry Hall had built it to hide his ill-gotten gold. And this notion, it seems, is the most plausible as we shall soon see. Plus, the fact that Mary Otis was as surprised as the carpenter to discover the secret panel would seem to confirm that it was there before the Otis', leaving only the Browns or Hall as the possible builders. (Although Hawley may have corrected himself over time—in the 1936 description of Geneva homes he conclusively says that Hall moved into the completed mansion in the spring of 1835, shortly before his death, but that General Otis built the vault personally and that the laborers who constructed it were the ones to gossip).

Whichever story is true, an interesting article appeared years later that seems to close the door on the tunnel scenario for good: while building the Belhurst Castle, workers had recalled the stories of the underground tunnel and of countless wealth in gold, silver and other valuables. But the excavators failed to discover any tunnels except "for one made by squirrels, by the appearance of which it is supposed that it has been the runway of a small army of these little creatures for many years."[12]

And so, we finally come to the third reportedly Haunted House on the property, which of course is the Belhurst Castle. It is here that reports of seeing the Lady in White are heard for the first time. One of the most colorful tales comes from Margaret Wilson, the daughter of Alec Ramage who was a groundskeeper and chauffeur for the Collins' (between 1923 until Carrie's death in 1926, at which point the Ramage family stayed on as caretakers until a new owner moved in). Margaret relates that her mother, a very practical and down-to-earth lady, one day told her that she had awoken one morning to see an apparition floating through the high windows in her bedroom (windows which cannot be opened). The woman wore what looked like a wedding dress, and as she descended, she carried a long veil flowing behind her, which she presented to Margaret's mother before vanishing.

---

12. *Geneva Gazette*, May 25, 1888.

There are also other strange events, as related by several staff members. Guests report all manner of strangeness: room eight's showers unexpectedly turn on and off. In another room, which had been the nanny's quarters, a lady is heard singing soft lullabies in the night.

Guests complain in the morning about screaming and playing children in an adjoining room, only to find out that the room was empty. (Pregnant guests especially complain about this, and this room was once used as a nursery for children while their parents socialized).

A water heater explodes while a group of out-of-towners attempt a séance. (Séances during the Golden's time were forbidden after this incident, and today people are strongly "discouraged" from attempting one.)

Several guests report seeing the old caretaker, Dick O'Brien, deceased since 1972, walking the stairs or sitting in a chair, wearing his favorite hat or carrying his wood-chopping ax.

Visitors complain of upstairs guests moving furniture in the middle of the night. Again, it is discovered in the morning that the room above was empty—but during the old casino days that room had contained the roulette wheel and gambling tables—which were frequently moved around after closing time.

A psychic visiting from Texas and staying in Carrie Collins' old suite reported the overwhelming impression that a previous owner adored the view from the verandah.

A spirit seen by the maids supposedly haunts the laundry room. Bartenders report instances of glasses and bottles mysteriously flying off their shelves.

And in one of the oddest scenarios, the wait staff arrived one morning after setting up for a large banquet only to find all the napkins and tablecloths tied in knots on the chandeliers above the tables.

These are just some of the stories coming from the Belhurst Castle in recent times, and to make any judgments at this point would be premature, not having met all the players in this drama. In the conclusion of this work, several theories will be presented that might tie all these experiences together, but throughout the rest of the chapters, I will attempt to be as objective as possible, sticking only to the facts and letting the reader draw what conclusions might come.

But for now, we return to that most popular legend, that of the Spanish Don and his Opera Singer, which has remained unchallenged since 1936. To repeat the old adage again, truth *is* sometimes stranger than fiction—in this case, much stranger—and while slightly less romantic, it is intensely passionate and dramatic in its own right.

In 1830 a ship was setting sail from England, bound for a land already rich in mystery and beauty; and traveling on that ship would come the seeds of a legend that would grow and endure in the minds of Genevans for over 170 years...

3

The Bucke-Hall Affair and the Making of a Legend

"Pay no attention to that man behind the curtain."

—<u>The Wizard of Oz</u>

He sat at the table, holding fast to the cabin wall as the ship rocked back and forth. Outside, the wind howled and the rain beat down in sheets on the Atlantic. He took a sip of whiskey, shuddered and wrapped his cloak around him tighter. Hooded candles flickered in the cabin, the largest room he could purchase for this voyage, yet still so cramped for three people and all their important possessions.

A thud struck the door, and it heaved open, admitting a cloaked woman and a young boy.

"William Nathaniel!" shouted the man. "I told you to stay below."

The boy backed up, into the arms of the drenched woman who pulled back her hood. Beautiful blue eyes that held such a range of emotions gazed up under tassels of stringy blond hair.

"William," she said to the man, out of breath. "There's been an accident."

William Henry Bucke bolted upright and reached for his son. "Is he all right? Isabella, what happened?"

"No," she interrupted. "Not to him. Another woman. One of the passengers. She…fell. Tripped on the deck and dropped into a hatch."

Bucke looked up at her, releasing his grip on young William Jr. "And this is our concern why?"

Isabella closed her eyes, taking a deep breath. "I had just been talking to her, she was such a dear soul, and—"

"No!" Bucke growled. "We do not talk to people on this trip. I thought I had made that clear."

"Yes, but—"

"No one! Not until we reach America, not until we're safely away."

"But William, if they want to track us, they will." Isabella took several steps into the cabin, then slumped onto a wooden chair beside the bed as the ship rocked again. "You were not careful."

"I was," he insisted, glaring at her.

"No, Scotland Yard is good. They can track your contacts. See that you went to the Land Offices and find out where it was you had been inquiring about. How much you offered, and the arrangements you made."

He shook his head. "I'm using an alias, and so are you. They won't know, unless there's more of this foolish talk to other passengers."

Isabella sighed, wiping away the rain, or tears, from her face. William Jr. moved to a corner and reached for some dry clothes. "She may not walk again," Isabella said.

"Who?"

"The woman who fell. Emma."

Bucke sighed. "Is there no one to look after her?"

"She has an uncle, James. He is heartbroken, and his agony is just as great. He blames himself, and—"

"Then she is in good hands with this uncle. Stay away from her."

Isabella stood up quickly, tying her cloak around her. She took a bottle of whiskey and some fresh towels and one of her dresses.

"What are you doing?" Bucke asked, meaning to stand in her way of the door. Isabella spun and slipped past him with the ease of a dancer on stage.

"We have the means to help, and I intend to." She faced him at the door. "They are in the lower deck, cabin twelve, if you change your mind and wish to join me." And with that, she slipped into the night.

Bucke shuffled back to the desk and sat heavily, raising his face to the ceiling.

"Father?" the boy called. "When are we going back to London?"

"We're not, son."

"But, Mother—"

"Isabella is your mother now. And you'll make new friends where we are going, and you'll get proper schooling, and we'll have a great house with a beautiful view." He sighed, and in his mind he could see the scene back at the Covent Garden Opera Theater: poor Kimble rushing about yelling at his staff, demanding an accounting. Calling in the police, beginning the search for his ex-treasurer. Questioning his equally incredulous wife.

Kimble, he didn't feel concern for. The current offering was a huge hit, and the loss of one night's take was nothing compared to the history of trials the theater had weathered before. His wife, however, was another story. But her image was fading, and only

Isabella Robinson remained. She was all he could see, and here in the pounding rain half an ocean away from his home, he wondered if he had been blinded by her beauty and by the eloquence of her song.

Was he sailing heedlessly to his doom like Odysseus following that Siren voice to some tragic shore?

He took another gulp of whiskey, then forced a smile when he looked at the three boxes of cash, coins and valuables stored under the bed, and he turned to his son. "Remember boy, your name is Hall now. William Nathaniel Hall. I am Henry Hall, and we are just rich settlers from Europe making a new home for ourselves in Geneva."

He rose, put on a hat and grabbed his cane, engraved with a silver buck's head at the tip. "Stay here boy. I'm going to fetch your stepmother and save us from discovery."

◆   ◆   ◆

William Henry Bucke, his son William Nathaniel, and the woman named Isabella Robinson left from London on a steamer to the New World on May 10, 1830. Dr. Hawley made an exhaustive report on this affair, which he linked intricately to the Haunted House of his youth, and it was with great excitement that he came across diaries, notes, eyewitness reports, and an almanac of James Simons.

It was in those records that we learn of a close friendship that began on the long trip from England between Bucke, Isabella Robinson and the Simons'—James and poor Emma. James' niece Emma suffered greatly from that fall, and spent the rest of her days until her death in 1883, paralyzed but for one arm. "Her patience under her sad affliction was an example of marvelous Christian fortitude,"[1] Hawley writes. She is buried in Glenwood Cemetery beside James Simons, on whose plot also rests Admiral Verveer of the Dutch Army, who as we shall see, was the father of Simons' second wife.

The facts, as we have them, are that in this close friendship, eventually James Simons did learn of the events at the Covent Garden Opera Theater, and the reason for the flight of his new friends. By way of background, the Covent Garden was the most famous play house of its time in England, beginning operations in 1733; it was twice destroyed by fire, and once involved in massive public riots over price hikes to pay for financial concerns.

---

1.   G.M.B. Hawley, "Chronicles of Geneva," *Geneva Daily Times*, May 28, 1921.

William Henry Bucke was treasurer for a short time. (I was unable to determine for exactly how long, as the records are sketchy. In <u>The Annals of the Covent Garden Theater</u> two treasurers are named—for the period up until 1828 and then after 1835, but it is strangely silent about the 1830 period. English historians contacted in connection with the theater also had no answers). Regardless, Hawley relates that his informers, including an elderly Geneva attorney involved in the case, and Bucke's own son, having told the tale late in his life on a return visit to Geneva, confirmed the story. After a long hit run of a play, Bucke emptied the coffers of the theater and absconded with the evening's take, a considerable sum.

Illustration courtesy of the Mander & Mitchenson Theatre Collection, London.

He took with him Isabella Robinson, who it is said was either an actress on the stage, or the wife of one of the owners. Researching the theater, I found no connection between Robinson and the owner, who was Charles Kimble at the time; he was happily married and had an exceptional singer as a daughter (Fanny Kimble, who toured extensively, even to America).

Isabella, then, was likely an actress, one of exceptional beauty and talent. There were other prominent Robinsons on the stage at Covent Garden, but they performed earlier. Mary Robinson, who created the role of 'Perdita' from Shakespeare's *The Winter's Tale*, died in 1800, but her beauty captivated the Prince of Wales (later King George IV) who had her become his mistress, only to dismiss her later after buying her silence.

Then there was the famous Anastasia Robinson who lived from 1692-1755 and worked with Handel to create the role of Cornelia. She attracted the eye of another noble, Lord Monmouth, Count of Peterborough. He eventually married her in secret in 1722.

Isabella Robinson's entry in Simons' almanac states she was born in 1801, and her full name was Jane Isabella Letitia Sophia Robinson. As we shall see very soon, it is likely that being an actress, she took on the stage name of Robinson in deference to the great performers mentioned above.

In any case, it seems the predilection her namesakes had for attracting dangerous men continued. William Henry Bucke convinced her to leave with him and his newly obtained small fortune. He sent his butler to the London Academy where ten-year-old William Jr. was studying, and brought him to Liverpool where Bucke introduced him to Isabella, his new stepmother. (It is here that a confusion of pronouns in Hawley's article led to an unintended misinterpretation—for decades many thought that Bucke actually married his own stepmother, then introduced her to his son as such. However, from the actual notes and facts it is clear that he was introducing his son to a woman who was to be his new mother. Besides this, the fact that Isabella was only 29 years old at the time, and likely younger than Bucke, makes any other interpretation illogical.)

It is not conclusive as to whether Bucke ever married Isabella (although James Simons' journal makes it clear he believed her to be Bucke's wife). When Bucke arrived in Geneva, introducing himself as Henry Hall, he had Joseph Fellows make out the property to be held in a deed of trust for Isabella Robinson. Not Hall, and not Bucke. He also gave Fellows all of his money to invest, again in Robinson's name.

The three made quite a little stir in Geneva when they appeared in late 1830; they were well-vouched for, received like they were English royalty and accepted without question because of their "more than ordinary wealth". However, Bucke's behavior soon became increasingly strange. He grew paranoid, more reclusive, and was tight-lipped during the building of his new mansion. Ultimately, when it was completed, he even boarded up the windows of his "Hermitage".

After a time, the Halls saw no visitors other than James Simons, who lived first on a farm in the town of Benton in Yates County, a short distance south of Geneva. On September 10, 1834 Bucke-Hall drew up a will in "which his estate is devised to Joseph Fellows in trust for Isabella Robinson and his son, William Nathaniel Hall, share and share alike."[2]

A short time later, English creditors arrived in Geneva seeking a man named Bucke. He wasn't hard to find. In addition to the stir and distrust he created by his reclusiveness, he had all of his silver ornaments and items engraved with a buck's head, and earlier had taken pleasure in showing them off. Consequently, townspeople had begun referring to him as Bucke-Hall.

In an anticlimactic end to this affair, an "arrangement" was arrived at through a local attorney, and a settlement was issued that satisfied the creditors. The details of that settlement are not known, but it is possible that Bucke-Hall got away with most of his theft. Having kept nothing in his own name, he could have claimed he spent it all, and perhaps they weren't prepared to take his uncompleted house.

Irreparable damage was done, however, to Bucke's reputation. The bubble burst and the story leaked out. "This gave rise to misgivings and a ready acceptance thereafter of mystery based upon the dangerous result of knowledge of part of the truth. The mention of Bucke-Hall, and those who had been duped were ready to believe and probably to start anything—even stretch it a little."[3] Talk even sprang up that Bucke-Hall had dug a tunnel from his Hermitage down to the lake to escape pursuers from Scotland Yard.

From that point on, the Hermitage and the people who lived there were ostracized, and mystery surrounded them. Unfortunately there was little chance to make things right. In the summer of 1835 in a fit of anger, prone to rage as he often was, Bucke-Hall chased his son around the property in order to chastise him with his cane. He tripped on a log and broke his leg.

The injury developed into blood poisoning, and given his typical paranoia plus the events of recent months, he refused to send Isabella for medical assistance. He died within days. The newspapers have only one line to say about his passing: that he "died at his home near this village, Henry Hall".[4]

---

2.   Ibid.
3.   Ibid.
4.   Ibid.

Now the story gets even more interesting. Isabella immediately sent William Jr. to get James Simons, and upon his arrival they sold the house and the property to Joseph Fellows for $10,862 (a marked increase due to the mansion).

Isabella and James were married shortly afterwards. All kinds of speculation can occur here regarding just when the interest between these two began, perhaps envisioning that their friendship on the Atlantic-crossing held the start of an affair. It is clear that Bucke-Hall adored Isabella to the point of obsession, but one has to wonder if she did in fact ever marry him, and whether his affection was ever fully returned.

One could also wonder at the timing of his death, so shortly after a will was created granting Isabella much of the estate, but with the facts at hand, of course any conclusions would be mere speculation and are likely just coincidence.

In 1842 the son, William Nathaniel Hall, drew up a settlement with James and Isabella Simons where these facts were related and he released himself of any interest in his father's estate. He left for California, and ultimately wound up in Gold Hill, Nevada where he was known as Judge William N. Hall. He was also a hardware merchant for a time. In 1890 he returned to Geneva briefly to meet with James Simons. In his will of 1891, James Simons grants to William Nathaniel Hall $2,000 plus his collection of silver spoons and teapots engraved with a stag's head (undoubtedly passed on from William Bucke's collection).[5] Ironically, according to Emmons, some of these ornaments were still about town in his day (the 1950s), a tangible reminder of Bucke's presence in the town's history.

Returning now to Isabella and James, their union did not last long. Isabella died just ten years later. In his Almanac, James Simons writes only: "My poor wife died March 15, 1846, aged forty-four years."[6] There was no record in Geneva for where she was buried, and it took the better part of the past year to locate her, a quest unto itself.

Almost as this book was going to print, I received a response to one of many queries in the neighboring towns, a note that yes, they did have an Isabella Simons—in the town of Benton, in Yates County. My wife and I made the trip to Benton, to see for ourselves, and after many hours back and forth on route 14, trying to find a street that no longer existed and a tiny plot of twelve headstones long since covered with trees and bushes, we took a chance on a side street. I

5.   The Last Will of James Simons, of the Village of Geneva, Ontario County, New York. April 23 1891.
6.   G.M.B. Hawley, "Chronicles of Geneva," May 28, 1921.

asked the resident of a house set back from the road and she merely nodded and pointed off to a nearby patch of trees.

"*Walking through thick groundcover, the scant light slicing through the trees gave the site an ethereal vision. And standing in the sunlight, straight as a flower reaching for nourishment from the light, stood Isabella's headstone. It was as if her grave, of all in this tiny secluded place, was the only resilient artifact left from that time, as the other gravestones, those of the Angus family, were worn and in disrepair. Perhaps this was a visage of her character, and what she was in life. And although we may have been her first deliberate visitors in over a century, maybe even more, it felt to us that she belonged here, in this sacred place along the lake, where her story and her life remain secluded and distant, but still attainable to those interested parties. We came here seeking the woman behind a legend, and we found much more.*"[7]

The next few weeks saw the rest of her story come to light. Working backwards and trying to figure out why she was buried in the Angus family plot, I soon learned with some surprise that she was the daughter of one David Angus from Scotland. David, already with eight children, had twins in 1801—Jane Isabella and William. His wife died shortly after this birth, and, unable to care for such a large family, he requested aid from his brother Walter, who ironically, had

---

7.   Journal of Amy Sakmyster, July 21, 2003.

come to America several years earlier at the suggestion of his friend Charles Williamson. Walter took on the children, as he had done for other family members. He was a very successful miller and entered into various trades; he sold his goods across several states and had a passion for travel and adventure.[8]

More on Isabella was not available, but we can speculate that perhaps she returned to Europe to look up her father; while there she entered the theater and found her way to London (and took on a stage name). And while in London, she met William Bucke, and at his request—offered up a suitable hiding place across the ocean: her childhood home.

In 1839 her father, David Angus, came over with the rest of his family to stay with Walter; so he had some time with his daughter before Jane Isabella died in 1846. Afterwards, David and Walter traveled some more and wound up in Minnesota, where they are buried.[9]

Some time after Isabella's death, James moved from Benton to Geneva. From 1852 until his death in 1897, Simons lived in a house near the College (the current Sigma Phi Fraternity House). He held several prominent positions—both in Benton and in Geneva, serving on local boards and as superintendent of Yates County.[10] He married again, in 1848, to Wilhelmina H.J. Verveer, born in the West Indies, daughter of Admiral Verveer of Holland who was stationed for many years in those islands, and who was commissioned to raise and train an army of local soldiers to fight for the Dutch. Their monuments, along with a stone for Emma Simons, are all at the same plot at Glenwood Cemetery, within sight of the Collins mausoleum.

Back at the Hermitage, confusion and mystery led to a crossing of stories. The rumors of the hidden passageway (the vault in the new mansion) came to be associated with Bucke-Hall because of his flight from England and the creditors who pursued him. While it is possible he may have designed such a vault (without the escape tunnel), the evidence points to the Browns and the Otis's as making use of it for more practical purposes.

So it is this sequence of events, this rich adventure which—it should be obvious by now—bears so many parallels to the folklore of the Spanish Don and the Opera Singer as to be inseparable, one and the same, with only minor changes occurring over time.

To review the major elements of the Opera Ghost legend: a rich Spanish gentleman became enamored with a beautiful opera singer. He left his wife for her,

---

8.   Stafford S. Cleveland, <u>The History and Directory of Yates County</u>, Penn Yan, 1873.
9.   Ibid.
10.   Oliver House Records.

stole a small fortune and fled across the ocean. They were pursued. He built a house overlooking Seneca Lake. His pursuers found him. He fled and his lover died in the retreat to the lake.

On the other hand we have what is known to be fact: the story of William Henry Bucke (Hall), which can be summarized exactly as above, except we need to substitute the word 'English' for 'Spanish', and at the end, it is he and not the opera signer who dies on the property.

Of course it's possible that *both* stories are true. There could have been, forty or fifty years before Bucke-Hall, the actual events as Carmer relates, but that would beg the favor of incredible coincidence. For two nearly identical dramas to occur in Europe, and then have both fleeing couples drawn to this one spot, out of all the possible escape locations? Could Geneva actually be some kind of magnet for opera singers on the run?

Disregarding that doubtful scenario is the only logical choice. However, before we rush to acceptance of the Bucke-Hall story as the one that evolved into the Carl Carmer legend of today, before we risk collapsing a very romantic tale that we all may desire to accept, it is necessary to examine a few more points that strengthen this interpretation.

First, as mentioned earlier, the history of Geneva was well-catalogued by George Conover in his works of the 1890s, E. Thayles Emmons in his <u>Story of Geneva</u>, and by G.M.S. Hawley who authored volumes of local historical studies. Conover, who fully detailed all the dealings of the Indian tribes and the English, French and American settlers, has no mention of a house built by a Spaniard. Emmons goes into lush descriptions of the first one hundred or so homes ever to be constructed in Geneva. Surely, if this one was built in the late 1780's (using Carmer's time frame) and its foundation visible even today, it would definitely have made mention in these works. (Not so unusually, notes are made repeatedly of Bucke-Hall's Hermitage cobblestone foundation being visible still, and of the Collins' need to seal over the well and cut through the foundation).

More damning, however, is that Hawley, an avowed obsessive regarding this property, the Haunted House legend, and all inferences involving the underground tunnels, having sought them frequently during his youth, never mentions this Opera Ghost legend. And even more alarming is that with his discovery of the Bucke-Hall affair and its obvious parallels, if the other legend did exist at the time I have to believe Hawley would have immediately pounced on the connection. But by his silence we are forced to admit that the legend was not in existence as late as 1921 when he wrote these facts about Bucke-Hall.

So, it is clear that sometime after 1921 and before 1936, the story of Bucke-Hall was, as Hawley put it, *willing to be stretched at least a little.*

Noted folklorist Louis Jones wrote extensively on the observation that early communities were prone to attach more romantic twists onto some elements of factual history, daring to create for their own towns some identity to rival their European counterparts, with tales of tragic loves and high adventure.

It seems something of the sort may have happened here—perhaps a mingling of truth with contemporary literature. Washington Irving's tales of upstate NY (like *Rip Van Winkle* and *Sleepy Hollow*) were gaining popularity, and the bulk of his other writing concerned mythical Spanish heroes and cities, centering on dramas of magic, love and riches.

Or maybe, and this is a stretch but worth investigating, there was an individual who planned to create something of the Belhurst Castle who could benefit by a little intriguing mystery, a slight tweaking of fact to help add to the romance of the setting. In a later chapter we may meet such a character, but it is not necessary that someone intentionally morphed history into something else—rather, time and retelling might have done the same trick. And so, by the time Carl Carmer requested local tales of rich folklore, there was one to be found.

While the affair of Bucke-Hall seems undoubtedly to be the root of the current legend, it is surprising that although many people throughout the years have been aware of the history of this Englishman, there have been no attempts to link this story to that of the Opera Ghost. (I would think that the mention of the Opera House alone would have been sufficient to get the idea brewing.)

However, if it is accepted that this factual experience is the legend's basis, then we are left with a larger question.

If the opera singer, in this case Isabella Robinson, did not perish tragically under the property, then who *is* strolling those grounds late at night, pining away in a white dress and causing more than a few shivers among the vacationing guests?

4

The Queen of the Castle

"In all the affairs of life, social as well as political, courtesies of a small and trivial character are the ones which strike deepest to the grateful and appreciating heart."

—Henry Clay (1777–1852)

She retires to her second floor suite, winded from her bike ride across the grounds. She fixes herself a glass of wine and strolls onto the balcony.

The front lawn in the pre-twilight hour is bustling with activity. Several guests from New York City are playing a spirited game of tennis on the new court, while on the pier Dell is proudly showing off his steamer to some local boating enthusiasts. The twenty-person craft is the envy of most in this region and Dell has been speaking of nothing else all winter but his desire to be out on the lake again.

A three-person band is playing soft violins while a few dinner guests arrive. And there's Hal, with his new ladyfriend, on summer break from College, strolling the grounds, making their way to the Poultry House. Doubtless the girl has never seen a Japanese Golden Pheasant before, much less two of the beautiful creatures.

Sighing, Carrie leans against the stone verandah ledge, sips at her wine and thinks back on the years it took to get here. The long winters in the cold Otis Mansion, the place everyone said was haunted; and all those curious folk inquiring whether any tunnels or treasure were found after the place was razed for this construction.

A thin smile crosses her lips as she takes in the view of the glorious lake, of her son walking hand in hand with a young love, and sweet Dell polishing the steamers' hull while the sounds of a tennis game and soft violins glide along the lake breezes.

Yes, she thinks. We did find treasure. Only it wasn't in some dank underground passage, but here, on the surface, waiting to be enjoyed.

◆   ◆   ◆

Carrie Moore Young was born in Cincinnati, OH on August 26, 1849. Her parents, John Young from New Hampshire and Caroline Moore from Ohio, had a son nine years earlier, Henry Clay Young, named after their ancestor, the renowned Senator from Virginia.

This family had considerable wealth as it was, but soon John Young was to be involved in the formation of a new company that would be extremely successful. In the Hamilton County archives for company listings, one can find that Theodore Royer formed the Royer Wheel Company in 1851. In 1856 the company ownership register included the names Joseph Simonton and John Young. Most likely Royer expanded and required additional capital, which came from these principals. The Royer Wheel Company specialized in the manufacture of carriage wheels, spokes, hubs and rims, and they used steam-powered equipment in the manufacturing process.[1] During the Civil War, the company's sales boomed as they provided wheels to the Union Army. Royer had a national reputation, thriving until the late 1890s, dying out only with the coming of the automobile.

In 1875 Carrie's brother, Henry Clay Young, succeeded as president and held that position until 1883. There is no mention of what happened to John Young, and even his obituary records are lacking (although the 1870 census lists him as being 'Pres. Of—National Bank', and his personal estate was valued at $500,000). It may be safe to say that upon his death he left his son a stake in the Royer Company, and left his daughter well-funded to pursue whatever dreams she imagined.

On March 4, 1868 Carrie married Samuel V. Harron, who was, or was soon to be, an officer of Royer as well. The 1870 U.S. Census lists his occupation as 'Patent Agent'. By the time of the 1880 census, Samuel Harron is recorded as living in New York City and having the title of Secretary of the Royer Wheel Company.[2] Carrie and their nine-year-old son Hal are listed in his Household, along with a servant named Lily Smith, and—curiously—another gentleman named Louis Dell Collins.

Mr. Collins was born in Rose Valley, NY in 1852. He was a clerk in the wholesale drug business in New York City for seventeen years (up until 1885). It is quite likely that the drug firm he worked for was that of Shieffelin &

---

1.   Hamilton County Historical Company Records.
2.   1880 U.S. Census.

Co.—since a native Geneva resident named Lewis Clark, according to his bio in Emmons's <u>Story of Geneva</u>, worked at that same company for twenty years. Clark returned to Geneva in 1887, just two years after Carrie and Mr. Collins would move there.

Again, if I may engage in some speculation. The story goes that Carrie M. Young/Harron had heard all these wonderful tales of the beauty of this spot on Seneca Lake, but I always wondered from whom? It may not be much of a stretch to assume that Louis' co-worker had regaled them with tales of his scenic home, and her interest had been sparked enough to take a visit and see for herself.

At some time before the move and whatever led Carrie to leave her husband behind (and we can of course speculate there as well), she had been attending medical school, and had even attempted a singing career. She then referred to Louis Dell Collins as her 'manager', and when she arrived in Geneva in May of 1885, she introduced him as such when they went to the real estate firm of G.W. Graham. She was shown the Otis Grove property, asked the price, and within ten minutes, closed the deal.

The newspapers at that time were naturally excited and curious. The 'Otis Place' had been vacant for seven years. A year after Carrie moved to Geneva, in November of 1886, the editor of the *Geneva Advertiser* expresses satisfaction at being given a tour of the grounds by one Mr. Thomas Hoult. Hoult was a part-time caretaker of sorts, a carpenter by trade, and he was hired by the Otis's first, to put "the cottage in its present shape. It is of English design and from its large bay window a fine view of the lake is afforded and of the hills beyond".[3] The cottage, the old Hermitage, was cleaned up and made livable for Carrie and Louis as they planned what to do with the property.

The paper reports Mr. Hoult, along with Mr. Collins' good management, "has taken all the wildness out"[4] of the grove. In 1886 or early 1887, Carrie divorced Samuel Harron, and on June 6, 1888 she married Louis Dell Collins. Up until that time the couple had been busy on the property. Dell (as Carrie called him) took an active role (and this may be where his title as 'manager' fits in). He managed the property, improving the grounds, adding a tennis court, and then building a boathouse in which they stored their "neat steam yacht, a New York model, propelled by a gasoline engine, which will easily carry 20 persons."[5] Several years later this boathouse was unfortunately destroyed in a fire. It took

---

3.   *Geneva Advertiser*, November 23, 1886.
4.   Ibid.
5.   Ibid.

four days for it to burn completely, and one can only imagine the emotions Dell must have felt during those days. A barn and stables were on one corner of the property; the barn also later burned down.

Next, Mr. Collins planned and built a poultry house; it was made out of brick and plaster, heated with a Furman Steam Boiler, and had wire screen partitions for each breed of fowl. The papers of the day state that the Japanese Golden Pheasants and the cockerel were worth traveling miles to see.

It was during this November, 1886 trip to the property that the editor was told of Mrs. Harron's plans to raze the old house to the ground and begin construction on a new structure. The editor compliments Carrie as "well deserving of all the comforts that nature and art can bring to surround her. She has the happy faculty of making her callers feel entirely at home, although the call be most informal and accidental."[6]

---

6.   Ibid.

Carrie M. Harron / Collins——Photo courtesy of The Geneva Historical Society

So the old Hermitage was destroyed on May 25, 1888 and construction began on what the townspeople only knew would be a three-story mansion, and would "doubtless be the finest structure of this kind in Western New York."[7] Carrie and Dell hired noted architect Albert Fuller to design the mansion. Fuller (1854-1934), had, at the turn of the century, developed many of Albany's landmark buildings, including the Fort Orange Club, the University Club and the Harmanus Bleecker Library, as well as School #10—which in 1999 made the list of the National Trust for Historic Preservation's most endangered national landmarks. (Ironically, it was being threatened by the construction of an Eckerd drug store in its place, the drug chain in which was associated, as we will see, a later owner of the Belhurst.)

For the Collins' mansion, Fuller used entirely Medina stone, designed three large stories in the form of an English castle, with towers and turrets, and an arched driveway with a large round alcove facing the east. Fuller used "Richardsonian Romanesque" design, the style named for Henry Hobson Richardson (1838-1886), which is based on French and Spanish Romanesque precedents of the 11th century. "It is characterized by massive stone walls and dramatic semicircular arches, and a new dynamism of interior space."[8] The style influenced others beside Fuller, including Chicago architects Louis Sullivan and Frank Lloyd Wright. City Hall in Syracuse and Boston's Trinity Church are other notable examples.

The firm of W.G. Dove did the masonry work with thirty-five men, while Persons & Siglar did the woodwork with approximately twelve men. Margaret Wilson recalls the story that Carrie brought in German apprentices from overseas whose sole job was to sharpen the tools used by the masons. The *Geneva Gazette* in September 1889 reported that the woodwork, which had begun in the spring, was not yet completed. "The magnitude and excellence of the work can be judged from this fact."[9]

The materials were all imported from Europe or Central America, and the furnishings as well, including gold-plated spigots, Honduras mahogany and crystal chandeliers. The chandelier in the dining room (sold off sometime after Carrie's death) was a duplicate of one in the White House.[10] Rumors ran that the Castle cost $475,000 to build, although a 1926 valuation appraises it at only $68,000. (Recalculating those figures in 2003 dollars, the former amount seems more

7.   *Geneva Gazette*, May 25, 1888.
8.   Digital Archive of American Architecture.
9.   Ibid., September 24, 1889.
10.   Interview with Margaret Wilson, August 2003.

likely—as $475,000 at 1888 would be comparable to $12.9 million today, whereas the claimed 'appraised' amount would only be $1.3 million, which seems far too low given the workmanship and the quality of the materials, plus the location.) An article at the end of 1888 reports that some locals, upon learning of the design plans, were disappointed that such a magnificent project would not include fountains or wading pools.

During the construction, which lasted nearly three years, only one serious accident occurred. Indeed, Mr. Dove of the masonry-contracting firm had been overheard congratulating himself that the heavy part of his work (lifting immense stones up some sixty feet) had been completed without serious injury to anyone. However, during the first week of December 1889 Jacob Hoffmeister from Rochester and his friend Mr. Frank from Waterloo fell while working on the kitchen roof. It was a drop of some twenty-five to thirty feet. Hoffmeister, 31 years old and married only seven months earlier, had broken ribs and serious internal injuries, and he died several days later at a neighbor's home. His wife had just enough time to make it to Geneva and be there for his last moments. Frank was shaken up, but not seriously hurt.[11] It was later reported that he "went insane", although whether this was from an unseen head injury, the tragic death of his friend, or something else entirely, is unknown.

In February 1891 the work was almost completed and the papers reported that Mr. and Mrs. Collins would move into the mansion "in early Spring." Carrie would soon be residing in the second floor suite, with a view of the grounds and the lake from one of the most elegant homes in the region.

And so, just over a century after a previous 'Castle' constructed by the native people had been destroyed by the Colonial Army, a new Castle was born in its place, keeping an abbreviated version of the more recent name, "Belhurst".

Carrie and her husband were "sufficient to themselves", living in what amounted to a self-contained city (with its own dock, tennis court, conservatory, stables, barn and icehouse), but they did take an active role in socializing, and were always open for visits and tours. Dell actually was very busy outside of his Belhurst activities. Apart from being an officer in the 3rd Brigade, he continued his passion for designing buildings, creating the Elks building and the Collins Music Hall. He was the president of Collins Iron Works in Phelps for many years and a charter member of the Geneva Lodge of Elks, as well as a member of the Old Guard from New York City. Additionally, and this apparently was a serious issue at the turn of the century, he was a volunteer member of the 'Bicycle

---

11.   Ibid., December 6, 1888.

Police'. The role of these bicycle-riding lawkeepers was to control reckless speeding by other bicycles—clearly a danger to pedestrians and themselves.[12]

Photo courtesy of The Belhurst Castle

Louis Dell Collins died on July 5, 1939. He had grown deaf by at least the early 1920's, and Margaret Wilson relayed several amusing stories about how Carrie would have to repeat herself many times to get her point across. He had no children, but his nephew, Arthur H. Vanderburg, became Senator of Michigan in 1928. Vanderburg was a staunch isolationist at the start of the WWII, then jumped in with strong support after Pearl Harbor; he was also instrumental in drafting the United Nations charter, establishing NATO and the FDIC.

Carrie's son from the Harron marriage, Hal, went to school in Geneva, and in various registers we read of his honors and scholastic achievement, studying ethics and history.

It seems Carrie never did practice medicine, but according to the 1911 Geneva Directory, she was on the Board of Directors for Geneva City Hospital. According to her grandson and confirmed by Margaret Wilson, she kept a skele-

---

12.   E. Thayles Emmons, <u>The Story of Geneva.</u>

ton in her closet—a study-aid from college anatomy classes. It's something Hal Jr. kept and showed people, occasionally with great humor, asking them if they wanted to see his grandmother's skeleton.

At some point Carrie brought to the grounds a bust of Henry Clay, which still stands at the Belhurst today, looking out over the lawn towards the lake. It was sculpted by the noted artist, Caroline Shawk Brooks, who was born in Cincinnati just 9 years before Carrie, and may have been friends of her family. Caroline's father, Samuel H. Brooks, was the inventor of the first steam engine.

Margaret Wilson relates that Mrs. Collins was an "environmentalist" before that word even took on meaning. She had strict rules that all life on her property was to be respected. Nothing could be killed. She took great pains to keep the trees perfectly pruned, the grounds immaculate, and all the wildlife, including what she imported, was treated as sacred. At the same time, she was a vain woman in many respects; she had her main living quarters done with full length mirrors, and she was always covered with diamonds when meeting people.

Photo courtesy of The Belhurst Castle

Carrie Collins died in 1926 while in Savannah, GA. She is interred in a great white stone mausoleum in Glenwood Cemetery, Geneva, along with Dell, her grandson Hal, and Henry Clay Young, her brother. They are atop a hill that possibly, years before the trees grew to their current height, could command an impressive view encompassing the distant hills across the lake, almost all the way to her Castle.

Collins Mausoleum, Glenwood Cemetery

In her will Carrie states that she gives "to my grandson Hal Ingham Young Harron and to his heirs forever, my home, 'Belhurst'…and all the furniture and other articles therein, and all my other real property."[13] Additionally, she had over $650,000 of assets (primarily in Dun & Bradstreet Stock). Louis Dell Collins received a $75,000 trust fund in the hands of the attorney who was advised to invest it and pay Dell only the net income from the fund, and only until either his death or re-marriage, in which case the remainder would be paid to her son and grandson, in equal parts. The rest of her wealth was to be likewise invested, with payments of net income made semi-annually to Hal and Hal Jr. until her grandson was thirty years of age, at which time he would receive it all to do with as he liked.

This amount of sudden wealth, for a young man like Hal in the roaring 20's, was too much. According to Wilson, he spent money like water, and went "a little wild". He only lived in the castle a short time before making an arrangement for a lease to Cornelius Dwyer (after the short-term residency of the Parmalees, who as we saw before, broke their lease and left the house within two months

---

13.   Will of Carrie M. Collins, Ontario County Records, Canandaigua, NY.

claiming the place was haunted). Hal is recorded as living in London and Bermuda, and at one point he may have been a naval officer in WWII. He died in 1986.

Carrie is gone, but her legacy remains; her vision and her dreams have stayed behind, encased in stone and ingrained upon this scenic landscape for generations to enjoy…

…and for others to enhance.

For the next Lord of the Castle had his own plans…

5

Belhurst's Heyday and the Reign of Dwyer

"When I sell liquor it's called bootlegging. When my patrons serve it on Lakeshore Drive, it's called hospitality."

—Al Capone

"I'm wiped out," he said after Mr. Wheeler left with a big smile on his face. The mahogany door closed softly, and the footfalls creaked heavily outside, down the stairs.

Heavy with the last of my money, young Cornelius Dwyer thought, rubbing his fingers through his thick red hair. Eight-hundred dollars. "The last buffoes I had." He glared at the shiny roulette wheel and that little ball, resting defiantly in number 27.

"Winners at roulette always come back to lose," he muttered, reflecting on what Uncle Luke Smith told him just a few weeks ago when he looked him up in Rochester asking for some advice. Dwyer had driven up in his Cadillac wearing the same clothes, the only clothes that he owned after losing everything in that damn stock market crash (except for his prized car which he had wisely hidden in the woods). Old Luke told him—"you don't need money, all you need is a roulette wheel."

Sure, Dwyer thought, his eyes glazing over, mesmerized by the twinkling lights in the silver wheel, reflecting the soft ambiance from the crystal chandelier overhead. He took a deep breath, tasting the bittersweet cigar smoke, hanging thick in the air like a used shroud.

Thoughts ran through his head about how to sneak off from this place, escape the lease he just signed with that nice rich kid, and flee across the country with his Cadillac.

That's all I really need, he thought. Money comes and goes, but a good car…one of those will treat you right. He sighed, got up wearily and walked to the balcony. He stared out over the lake and watched the twinkling stars as they watched him back.

Wheeler's Ford was driving away in a hurry, turning onto Main St. now. In Dwyer's mind, Uncle Luke's words whispered softly: "winners always come back..."

Something rustled behind his neck—a touch maybe, a lingering caress across his shoulders as if the wind offered him strength.

Dwyer closed his eyes and stood up straight. Taking a fresh cigar from his inside suit pocket, he leaned against the ledge, lit the tip, and took a deep, deep breath.

The smoke that puffed out in lazy rolling clouds did little to conceal the smile underneath.

◆   ◆   ◆

That gentleman did come back. They all did, returning to the scene of their winnings, and the odds and statistics were against them. Luke's advice came through for Dwyer, who had run his own most desperate gamble early in 1933, betting on the successful combination of fine dining, fancy splendor, and a little upstairs "divertissement"—as he called it.

Cornelius Dwyer was born in 1890 in Lyons, NY. At the age of fourteen he got thrown out of Catholic grammar school, reportedly for tearing the collar off of a nun. A seventh-grade dropout, he found work in the Lyons yards of the New York Central railroad, cleaning out locomotive fire boxes. Staying in the railroading business, he went on to firing a freight engine on the Auburn road for ten years, but eventually he came to believe there had to be an easier way to make money than shoveling coal.[1]

He had seen other pool rooms and gambling parlors, and was tantalized by the patrons and the games and the sense of the high life. His first enterprise was to set up his own gambling room in Lyons. He started with a dice game, then branched out during prohibition to running ale and whiskey down from Canada; he did this while also working as a policeman, then later as a detective.

The money came in, more than he ever imagined. He opened other gambling halls and casinos—plush establishments in Saratoga Springs, NY, in Hollywood, FL and in French Lick, IND. He ran card games, roulette, and racetrack betting. He had car hops and bell captains, and every finery imagined.

In the late 1920s, the game started to get complicated. Mob affiliations were springing up at most casinos, but Dwyer was able to stay isolated. "They never tried to muscle in on me. I knew them all, but they left me alone. There was

---

1.   *New York Times*, September 6, 1972, Michael T. Kaufman "Ex-Gambler, 82, Spins Back Wheel of Time".

enough for them all."[2] No, the big problem for Dwyer was corruption—the pay-offs for protection. Political bosses were one thing, but then you had to pay off the cops to look the other way; and soon that brought out more and more officials looking for their share. He had to cover a whole range of city, county and state workers, in addition to contributing generously to both political parties. He also had to hire "heavy men"—vacationing New York City detectives—to protect his customers from thieves.

It got so bad that he almost had to close the Piping Rock Casino in Saratoga; he was paying $20,000 for the racing season, and that amount on top of it for payoffs. He was saved at one point by bringing in some top entertainers, including jazz legends Sophie Tucker (the "First Lady of Show Business") and Vincent Lopez. And of course, it didn't hurt to win some high stakes either. His most memorable game: beating "John Hay Whitney, millionaire industrialist, publisher, philanthropist and sportsman, out of $52,000 playing a card game called 'Hazzard'."[3]

Things were turning around, business was good and the dream was coming true for Cornelius Dwyer, a self-avowed kid from the wrong side of the tracks whose father came to this country during the Irish Potato Famine.

Then came October, 1929. The Stock Market Crash. Dwyer was heavily invested, and lost it all. He had to sell all the casinos, his house, everything but the clothes on his back. Oh, and yes—his black Cadillac.

That he hid, and kept. And in time, he bought a new one. And another new one. Every year since 1922 he bought a new Cadillac, consistently picking the finest, most luxurious model. "I generally stick to something if it's a good thing,"[4] he said once when asked about his Cadillac passion. It was a motto he stuck with throughout his life and career.

For the next few years Dwyer struggled to get back on his feet. He worked as a bartender in Syracuse for a time, but eventually he was drawn back to the game.

With just enough money to try another venture, Dwyer ventured from Lyons to nearby Geneva, intrigued by the Belhurst Castle, standing in a wooded estate of forty acres sloping gently to the lake. (Years before, he had met the Collins' on occasions when he had run deliveries of pop from a concession store in Lyons.[5]) Driven by the comforts of his past establishments and his drive to return to that

---

2.   Ibid.
3.   *Democrat & Chronicle*, 1982.
4.   *Finger Lakes Times*, Nov. 11, 1971
5.   Interview with Dr. Kovach, Aug 20, 2003.

sense of wealth and splendor, he wanted to create the region's finest eating place, with of course—a little gambling included.

In 1933 Hal Harron Jr., who had not been at the Castle long, had been traveling frequently and looking to part with the property. When Dwyer approached him, a deal was easily made for a lease (which he would eventually buy out in the mid-1940's). Dwyer took a chance, hoping to quickly draw people in to the class and upscale vision he would create.

He bought a roulette wheel with $500 from a contact of his uncle's—a police captain who got it in a raid. Dwyer put it in a beautiful second floor room, and he was in business. He did lose that first night—all the money he had left was gone, but he won it back, and much more.

During this period Belhurst Castle became known as the Belhurst Club. Men and women came from all over the state, and then from all areas of the country. A nationally known food critic, Miss Clementine, wrote an ecstatic column on her experience at Belhurst for the *New York Herald Tribune* (which Dwyer proudly hung on the wall), and James Thurber, famed humorist of the *New Yorker*, was a regular patron. E.G. Robinson and James Cagney were occasional guests. The word spread. It became a favorite eating place for socialites and famous people like writer George S. Brooks and Notre Dame's Jim Crowley.

Dwyer's rich contacts and friends from his days at Saratoga Springs and the other casinos all made visits to Belhurst; they were industrialists, sporting characters, leaders in business and advertising.

He had entertainment again, fantastic food, liquor and gambling. The Sampson Naval Base across the lake provided his largest base of customers, and the weekends saw Belhurst full of officers and sailors, doctors and nurses. Three evenings a week he had entertainment provided by Art Dwyer on the horns and "Pop" Curry at the piano, along with another drummer. He even had an obscured road running up the cliff from Seneca Lake, used to bring in the liquor shipments from Canada—and this too may have added to the legends of the secret tunnels.

Through it all, Dwyer never ran afoul of the law—except once, before his arrival at the Belhurst. In 1931 he was arrested for possession of illegal alcohol after a party. He paid a $100 fine, and that was that.

In Geneva, the payoffs continued during the prohibition days and beyond. $5,000 was a standard annual contribution, paid to both political parties (a little more to the ones in office). Also, he had to make sure to contribute generously to the local charities. In Geneva his annual donations were second only to a rich steel executive. He called it "Hell Insurance, because his past performance chart was against him."[6]

The gambling days continued until 1951 when the U.S. Senate, under the Kefauver Commission, started cracking down on organized crime. For fifteen months beginning in May 1950, the nation was riveted to the publicly aired hearings exposing the 'enemy within', and they learned of the power and the reach of criminal organizations. Since the mob was heavily into gambling, operating most casinos, pool halls and illegal games, naturally anyone that had a casino was immediately suspected. Rather than risk the exposure and endure the pressure of subpoenas and penalties, Dwyer reluctantly closed down his gambling operation.

The Belhurst Club now focused solely on entertainment and fine dining, and one can only speculate on the nostalgia with which Dwyer had to close that door and spin the wheel no longer. Once asked about the gambling environment in his later years, Dwyer remarked that it would be too difficult (in the 70's), as the mob controlled everything and there was no chance for the little guy to get started and make something of it.

So Dwyer continued with what he did best, and the Belhurst Castle continued to thrive along with him. And like his affinity for new Cadillacs, Dwyer stuck to what he liked, to what worked. He had a schedule: 4a.m.-to-rise, 7p.m. to-bed, dinner at 3pm ("not 2:55, not 3:05", his half-brother Dick O'Brien once noted[7]), and two cocktails at dinner ("not one or one-and-a-half..."). With his later ailing health he was told to cut down to one drink (or 'daily pick-me-up', as he called it). After that news he remarked, "Jeez. I may become a prohibitionist".

He drank and used only La Tourraine coffee for thirty-eight years. At one point he smoked 25 or 30 of his trademark big cigars a day, but in later years he had to cut that down to 10. Every day at dawn he walked across the property, and in his later years, he would walk all the way to Glenwood Cemetery to the grave of his second wife, Margaret, who died soon after their wedding. Every winter until he could no longer drive, he would take his Cadillac and travel to Florida, California or Arizona.

He was always dressed in a sharp dark suit, starched white shirt, snappy bow-tie and a white handkerchief in his upper left lapel pocket.

His story was a one-in-a-million rags to riches tale, and it drew many interested parties eager to hear it. He was a man who loved to tell tales of the glory days, and he had no shortage of those cherished memories, so when he at last

---

6.   *Democrat & Chronicle*, 1982.
7.   *Finger Lakes Times*, Sep. 8, 1970.

consented to an interview from the *New York Times*, he spoke with "the candor of someone who has beat the statute of limitations."[8] He spoke freely on his years in the bootlegging, gambling and corruption business, and his story was an overnight hit.

After the 1972 article appeared, he started receiving calls and letters, requests for advice, television deals, congratulations from old friends and strangers, and of course requests for donations. He even got a call from someone at the Dick Cavett TV show. "All from two guys from the *Times* showing up one day, taking pictures and asking questions," Dwyer remarked after the article appeared and fame rolled in.[9] "Listen," he told the caller from the TV show, "the best stories about prohibition are the ones you can't tell."[10]

However, he did speak of one particular gambler, at his casino in Florida, who lost $100,000. The man had left his wife, who was a daughter in a wealthy publishing family, gambled away his money then fled without paying his debts. Dwyer sent a detective after him, who found the guy in the New York Athletic Club, broke and unable to pay a dime. So the detective went after the man's father-in-law, who, after making some threats to call F.D.R. himself, eventually offered $20,000 to make the issue go away.

Henry Clune, noted Rochester newspaper journalist and good friend, gave Dwyer the name of "The Squire", and in addition to usual "Red", he was often referred to as the "Squire of Belhurst."[11]

At some point, Dwyer sold ten acres of his property, and now that stretch of land has numerous homes on it, along either side of two thoroughfares which bear Dwyer's name. It was in this section that Dwyer would later live, constructing a new home in order to stay close to his beloved Belhurst and to retain a presence there after its sale.

During his time at the Belhurst, he was assisted by his "man behind the scenes", his half-brother Dick O'Brien, a colorful Irish character himself, who resided at the Castle along with his wife Eileen. O'Brien grew up with Dwyer in Lyons (where he was named 'champion basketball player of Lyons High School'). He later graduated from Notre Dame University and followed Dwyer to Geneva where they formed a successful partnership.

---

8. *New York Times*, September 6, 1972, Michael T. Kaufman "Ex-Gambler, 82, Spins Back Wheel of Time"
9. *Finger Lakes Times*, September 11, 1972.
10. Ibid.
11. *Democrat & Chronicle*, Aug. 9, 1970.

O'Brien was the "organization man" to Dwyer's magnetic social persona. He managed the restaurant business and casino operation early on, and efficiently supervised operations from a small side office next to the main dining room. Many guests made their way to his office first and then again at the end of the night, to get a firm handshake, a sincere grin and a few jokes to send them on their way.

He was remembered as a familiar sight to the neighbors of Belhurst Castle: "always in a sweatshirt and cap, carrying an ax or saw in his hand. He loved the outdoors, and could be seen chopping wood by hour and day, the wood that warmed the Castle fireplaces over the years."[12] His dog, a German Shepherd named Major, was his constant companion.

When O'Brien died from a sudden heart attack in the Castle on December 5, 1973, the papers lamented that his passing marked "the end of an institution." The Castle's big iron grill gate was closed and bolted for the first time in forty years. And Major's replacement, another German Shepherd named Shasta, lay just inside, mourning.[13]

Curiously, O'Brien's death came just two months after a re-assessment of the property occurred, something that hadn't been done in Dwyer's tenure there. This re-assessment resulted in a substantial increase in property taxes. O'Brien apparently reacted quite angrily to this news, and in a fit he grabbed a chainsaw and took down most of the twelve old trees lining the service road behind the Castle, stopping only at the plea of one of the neighbors.[14] It was an action out of character for a man devoted to the property, and one can wonder how the late Mrs. Collins would have reacted to such a desecration of her property. (And if one were superstitious, the timing of O'Brien's death might not seem so coincidental.)

Of course, there are those who say O'Brien hasn't really left at all, and he is still seen in his cap and sweatshirt, making his rounds, caring for the Castle that he loved and left only once (on a trip to his ancestral home in Ireland). A portion of the wall in the old cellar bears both signatures of Dwyer and O'Brien, along with the date they both signed it.

Cornelius "Red" Dwyer went on alone at Belhurst for only a few more years. In 1972, before O'Brien passed away, Dwyer was asked about someday letting go of the Belhurst, to which he vowed, "I'll never sell it. Not in a million years. It is

---

12. Ibid., Dec. 6, 1973.
13. Ibid.
14. Interview with Dr. Kovach, Aug. 20, 2003.

my home."[15] However, in 1975, without O'Brien by his side, and feeling his age, Dwyer began to seek out a new owner. He found an interested party who "would love the place as much as I have, and who will preserve its reputation for excellence in dining."[16] He passed the torch to Robert Golden on March 5, 1975, but wanted to remain close to the Castle. He moved into a house on Dwyer Drive, and continued his walks every morning, and ate at the Castle every night. "I still plan to be around the place quite a bit," he said. "I have a lot of friends and they'll be expecting to see me. I don't want to disappoint them."[17]

Seven years later, on January 7, 1983 the Squire of Belhurst "went out"—as he would have phrased it, at Geneva General Hospital at the age of 92. He had been in and out of the hospital for four years with various ailments, and had recently required round-the-clock nursing services at his home.

Dwyer had once told the president of Hobart College (who had asked for a donation), "I'm just a smuggler, a bootlegger and a gambler. And that's the way I want to go out."[18] But to those who knew him well, he was much more: a fantastic storyteller, a restaurateur, a celebrity, a husband and an uncle, and dear friend to many. "He made friends of the great, and became friends to the small."[19] In one of his last interviews he said, "I've done every damned thing you can think of...and for me, the livin' these past 40 years hasn't been too bad."[20]

---

15. Ibid., March 5, 1875.
16. Ibid.
17. Ibid.
18. *New York Times*, September 6, 1972, Michael T. Kaufman "Ex-Gambler, 82, Spins Back Wheel of Time".
19. Ibid.
20. *Finger Lakes Times*, September 11, 1972.

Photo courtesy of The Rochester Democrat & Chronicle

He is buried not far from Carrie Collins, near the property that they were both drawn to in an older, different age. He had tread carefully those age-worn mahogany stairs, walked those sacred lands high above the lakeshore, and breathed in the air of history. It was no wonder that Dwyer devoted so much time in his retirement to studying the history of Belhurst. One can only guess at what else he may have found, where his investigations took him, and what, ultimately drove him to search...

6

The Golden Era and Beyond

"Nothing endures but change."

—Heraclitus (535–475 BC)

When Robert Golden left Corning, NY and his comfortable position as President of Eckerd Drug Store, he was taking a gamble. Much like the man he was going to replace at the Belhurst Castle, Golden was bored with his current position and eager not only for a challenge, but a chance to get into his first love. "I was determined to get into the restaurant business," he remarked in his first year at the Castle.

He was 54 years old and he had four children (between 7 and 16 years old), so in some ways he was making a bigger wager than Dwyer did at his young age. Plus, in 1975 Dwyer wasn't looking to lease the property but to sell it at a good price (no details were disclosed as to the final offer, but it had been on the market for over $700,000).

Belhurst sale

Photo courtesy of The Finger Lakes Times

Robert and his wife Nancy had met Dwyer years before, during a trip to the Belhurst, and on March 5, 1975 he completed the sale, officially taking over on March 17. Golden moved in, setting his family up on the top two floors, but he always had it in mind to refurbish the upstairs rooms and convert them into guest suites; and when the children grew up a little more, he moved his family into a nearby home.

From the start, his goal had been to enhance the dining experience and to combine fine dining with a chance for guests to stay the night, a weekend or even longer in a place of great luxury and class. Golden had the experience to accomplish this. He had an uncle in the hotel business, "a big name for years".[1] And Golden worked in hotels all through high school and college, culminating in a

---

1.   *Finger Lakes Times*, March 5, 1975.

position as night manager at the Benjamin Franklin Hotel in Philadelphia while in college.

In 1986 he had finished refurbishing the upstairs rooms, and there were now eleven guestrooms available. During this work, and shortly after taking over from Dwyer, he expanded the menu, still focusing on Continental dishes, but he brought in a chef from the Hilton Hotel chain who had been a long acquaintance, and he hired a famous maitre'd.

He also made some interior decorating improvements to the woodwork and furniture—as he put it, "solely for enhancement of the present beauty of the castle."

By 1986 he had earned himself a title as well: "The Baron of Belhurst."[2] He had done something even Dwyer had not had the vision for: he had expanded. Where Dwyer was comfortable serving small parties and was at home with local friends and influential people, Golden thought bigger. In 1979 he added a 3,000 square-foot extension to the south side of the dining room. The new wing, of glass and batten-board construction, would only be used from mid-April through October, and it would be a screened-in, garden style area.

Soon, the Belhurst Castle was serving an estimated 100,000 customers annually (between dining and overnight guests)—60% of these were from out of town. It had a staff of over 50 workers; they were performing wedding parties, company banquets, and parties for busloads of senior citizens. Articles praising the dining and the accommodations sprang up in the *New York Times* and *Gourmet*, and the word was spreading.

In the few years before the garden-room addition, Golden had lamented that so many guests had to be turned away due to lack of space, and that was surely one reason for the need to expand. The other was financial.

Rising costs of heating, higher taxes and other expenses drove the necessity of more space. "Without additional seating capacity, long term, the restaurant cannot continue to exist."[3] Golden made this impassioned plea, the first of many he would later make, standing before the town planning board in April 1978. He got approval for it in short time.

But there were other fights ahead for Golden. Expansion led to opportunity, and he began to think bigger. Recalling perhaps the thrill of the large hotel operations, he began to plan a multi-million dollar inn and conference center on the northeast corner of the property. He had private funding lined up, and even had

---

2.   *Finger Lakes Times*, Feb. 21, 1967
3.   Ibid., April 19, 1978.

the interest of an architectural design firm (which had built three Irish Castles). All he needed was approval from the board.

What was to follow, in the late 1980's and into 1991, became a series of successes and setbacks to his vision. It was also an issue that severely divided the town. The Board first approved his request, only to have it appealed through petition by the neighbors. Then it was approved again, and blocked again. Golden made many impassioned pleas as to the benefit this expansion would have on the local neighborhood, the town of Geneva and the Finger Lakes area—the economic benefits plus the fact that again, without additional income the Belhurst might not survive. It was this threat of losing such an historic landmark that he effectively utilized, bringing in cost studies from outside appraisers detailing how rising expenses were leading to a desperate financial scenario.

Ultimately this issue, which had occupied so much of Golden's time and energy, seemed to have sapped what interest and strength he had left for the project. In 1992, acting on letters of interest in the property from Duane Reeder, he sold the Belhurst Castle and retired to Florida with his wife.

Photo courtesy of The Finger Lakes Times

Golden left the Reeder family a greatly expanded operation, a thriving, nationally known restaurant and inn, and a place of expanded beauty. During the Baron's tenure, the Belhurst Castle had grown into an attractive vacation spot, luring many for its scenery and proximity to fine wineries, to the nearby golf club, and to the watersports addition he had created. Seneca Lake Sports, Inc. began operations on July 31, 1991, with his daughter Kathy as President and Treasurer. Guests could now enjoy water-skiing, parasailing, or just touring the lake on a 30-foot pontoon boat that would have made old Louis Collins smile with envy. Golden even built a road to the lakeshore and the docks, cut through the 35-foot cliff.

After the Goldens left, the Reeders came in with energy and expansion plans of their own. In 1998 they opened a "sister property", the White Springs Manor, which has thirteen guestrooms in a stately refurbished Georgian Revival mansion. A second outbuilding, constructed by Dwyer in the '50's, was also converted into guest suites.

Today, at the restaurant and inn, expansion is continuing. As of July 2003, they have begun planting of a Belhurst Winery vineyard (the Winery is scheduled to open in May 2004). The initial planting is on 15 acres, with up to 60 additional acres to be planted within the next three years on White Springs Farm. Other plans include the construction of an upscale 20-room hotel, a place for wine tasting and retail sales, a new ballroom and a lounge on the Belhurst property.

There is even a new terrarium where guests can enjoy viewing pheasants and a stately peacock. (Duane Reeder decided to bring back these birds upon learning that Carrie Collins had been so fond of them.)

And as always, there is still room for intimate candle-lit dinners where the observant guest may notice the Japanese Golden Pheasants ingrained on the China, and some will make the historic connection. Maybe a little later, during cocktails in the mahogany-walled bar under that gold-framed portrait of Red Dwyer, they will talk with the locals about the powerful characters who created all of this.

Maybe they'll speculate on what remaining presences may yet cling to these walls, crouch in these hallways, and glide up these stairs—there, just beyond the suit of armor, up to the tower or to the verandahs where the previous Queen, Squire and Baron once walked in silent introspection of mysteries beyond understanding.

Maybe those previous owners closed their eyes, shut out the other senses, and just strained to hear the sounds that were just below range but always present. Is that the wind whistling past leaded windows, kicking up dust in an ancient ruin of a blind

cellar? Or is it the creaking of a rotted door to some once-magnificent, envious struc-
ture? Is that the hammering of boards over the windows by a frantic resident desperate
for privacy? Who is that singing—those soft, sweet tones, and those melancholy Italian
vocals? And is that the echo of someone's shovel, tunneling deep within the earth?

◆   ◆   ◆

There are stories here, everywhere you look. Some are harder to find than others, and some defiantly resist discovery. If nothing else, the Belhurst Castle, and
the property on which it rests, has a soul, and it is evident to anyone who visits.
And like most rich souls, this one wants to be shared; it sighs and patiently
encourages you to step in and become part of its history—to walk headfirst into
legend.

This place is, as Robert Golden once said, "something that will never happen
again in America."[4]

Photo courtesy of Neil Sjoblom Photography, Geneva, NY

---

4.   *Finger Lakes Times*, March 5, 1975.

7

Conclusions

"Has anything escaped me? I trust there is nothing of consequence which I have overlooked."

—Dr. Watson, <u>The Hound of the Baskervilles</u>

With the writing of any non-fiction, especially history, the author always has the fear that something has been recorded in error, misrepresented, or just plain missed. When dealing with events almost two hundred years old, this fear is compounded. Could some of the facts, as laid out here, be wrong? Of course. As we have seen, even in the recorded writings taken down close to the events as they happened, there were conflicting statements as to facts. Researchers are only as good as the source material (and their own use of logical deduction).

In all cases I have tried to be as logical as possible, and I hope I have at least captured the essence of the major periods involved; likewise I hope I have conveyed the heart of the stories that were there to be told.

Undoubtedly, the main quest in this writing was to unravel the colorful folktale of the Spanish Don and the Opera Singer. That, I believe, has been done effectively with the discussion of the Bucke-Hall affair. The similarities are too great to dismiss, and the chronological time frame makes it unlikely that a previous adventure of almost the same characteristics could have occurred.

The legends of the tunnel and the gold likewise have been dealt with through this revelation, and especially in light of the details of the cellar vault in the old Hermitage. While the dissolution of that folktale may be lamentable, it is still exciting to speculate as to how actual facts may have gotten stretched to such richly detailed romantic levels.

We know those tales likely started with the discovery of Bucke-Hall's lies in 1834. When the townspeople learned of his crime, his reclusiveness took on new meaning and speculation naturally resulted. He was building a new house, a huge home with winding staircases, towers and gables. All such houses had secret passages—surely his would too. Only, this man had something to put in those secret alcoves—great wealth that he had stolen from an Opera House. It is easy to see how this could have been stretched even farther—people were after him, so maybe while building this house he constructed an escape tunnel (since he was so close to the lake, a perfect getaway).

Next, over time, as the Brown home and later, the Otis Place, fell into ruin and scores of young treasure seekers came up empty, stories changed. The Belhurst Castle was built and the old place and its characters slowly faded from memory, perhaps only surfacing as inspiration for a retelling of the tale.

As mentioned earlier, other folklorists have noted the tendency in early American towns to accentuate local tales and dramatize them further to become the equals of their European counterparts. Maybe a few details are thrown in over the years, so that even after Hawley writes his article on the subject in 1921, it is not enough—or the connection isn't made. The story continues with a life of its own. Only now, it's not an Englishman who flees here, but a lordly Spanish gentleman. And he doesn't die in some unromantic, common way; no—his lover dies tragically and he winds up at a monastery.

It is this point in the Carmer tale that is revealing: it can almost be seen as a deliberate attempt to match Arthurian Myth, where Lady Guinevere, having tragically brought about the end of a kingdom through her illicit love for Lancelot, flees to a convent to live out her days. Much the same way we have our tragic hero, having yielded to carnal temptation, who ultimately brings down ruin on himself and the one he loves, and spends his remaining days at a monastery.

There is one other possible, although unverifiable, scenario that may have caused the change in the story. If I may speculate again, that sometime in the mid-1920's (shortly after Hawley's 1921 article), people began reporting a vision on the property and in the rooms of the Castle: a woman in white, ghostly and silent. She is seen enough to cause more than idle speculation among some of the elder members of Geneva, those old enough to remember scraps of earlier legends. Something about tunnels and buried gold. A passage to the lake, and an older house that once stood on this property, and oh yes…something about a beautiful opera singer.

Maybe it wasn't such a leap to relate a new ending to the actual story. If there really was a ghost of a beautiful woman in a white dress trapped here, and at other times singing was even heard, it only made sense that she was *that* opera singer. All that remained would be to guess as to how she died.

Of course this is just speculation, and I'll leave my final thoughts on this subject to my Afterword where it is better dealt with. However, keep in mind that time frame of the mid-1920's...

As for the rest of the stories here, again I hope I have conveyed them as accurately as possible, and I apologize where I have failed. The heart of this project quickly took on a life of its own, moving past the initial thesis on folklore, and focusing on the whole range of historical experiences at this property.

From its earliest mention, from the Fort at Kanadesaga and the concentration of Indian tribes, which set the notion that this land was powerful, sacred and full of promise, we moved on through other ages. The Williamson era of expansion and development, the ownership of Clark and later Fellows; Bucke-Hall and the mansion of mystery utilized by the Browns and Otis's. (It is the latter two chapters, of which so little is known, which I am most frustrated by, as I am sure there are equally dramatic experiences in that house during those four decades in which history, unfortunately, is silent). And then of course, there is the Carrie Collins era, the rise of the Castle and the expansion of a legend. Then Red Dwyer and the casino days, the glorious revelry in the defiance of prohibition and gambling laws, the enjoyment of luxury. And finally, Golden and Reeder, pushing inexorably outward, expanding with a bold echo of Williamson's dream two centuries earlier: to make more of the land, to create something lasting and memorable and worthy of a new order.

Afterword

"I may not have gone where I intended to go, but I think I have ended up where I intended to be."

—Douglas Adams (1952-2001)

It has been a long, strange and sometimes frustrating search, this quest to document the history of this historic landmark. Of course, at other times, it has been extremely rewarding—in ways I never thought possible. Discovering the events of the Bucke-Hall mystery, in the order in which they were to be found, was intensely exciting, and I imagine, much like the unraveling of a murder mystery.

There were numerous trips to cemeteries on wintry days, where I would scrape snow off of timeworn stones, and wonder at the names while wishing the dead could speak.

With great exhilaration, I felt as if the story tumbled into place with the discovery of the various facts in relation to the folklore. I had the Opera Singer connection, the romantic affair and theft of a great fortune, and the pursuers tracking the couple down to their new home. All that remained was to speculate as to how fact evolved into myth.

That accomplished, the other stories were just waiting to be studied, and when I did, I actually found just as much drama there as well. From Captain Williamson to Carrie Collins, from Dwyer to Golden, from tragedies like Emma Simons' story, to the happy love affairs like Carrie and Dell, Isabella and James, and the achievement of their dreams. These were incredibly complex characters that lived in exciting times and left behind something lasting and passionate for generations to enjoy.

But still, I am drawn back to that night three years ago. To the vision on the lawn, to the figure witnessed by many others before me. The inspiration for a legend. As I sit here now I feel oddly at ease with a certainty of what she is not. Given for a moment that what I saw was a real vision and not some sort of mirage or trick, then I feel strongly that she has been misinterpreted.

Perhaps it's a case of being in the right place at the wrong time. In the late 1920's memories remained of the story of Bucke-Hall and the beautiful opera singer from ninety years earlier. Then along come these visions, these sightings of a woman in white, and she is labeled at once as the ghost of this historic figure. The truth however, is that the only actual opera singer to flee to Geneva under such circumstances, Isabella Robinson, was not killed tragically here, but died in Yates County some ten miles away, where she is buried. Also, and more importantly, it doesn't appear that she had a great affinity for this place. She clearly had some wealth left after William Bucke-Hall's death, and could have stayed in the Hermitage with James Simons if she was attached so fondly to it (as the Opera Singer of the folktale had been).

But she immediately sold the place and moved away with James. No, the vision I saw gave me a different but very strong impression—and I don't know how exactly to convey this but to say that she exuded a sense of *attachment*. Of longing and desire to exist here. She was not projecting a sense of loss or sadness over a loved one; she was not desolate and broken-hearted after some tragedy. Rather, she seemed to fit in, to be one with the landscape.

It is this feeling, more than anything else, that leads me to the conclusion that this ghost, if indeed that's what it is, must be someone who adored this place. Someone who left her career, her husband, and her home in the city to be here, amidst these trees, in this grove overlooking this beautiful lake.

Someone who was fond of luxury, and someone who saw beauty in all things, and cared for the land, the trees, plants, and wildlife here as if they were her own flesh and blood. Someone who spared no expense to create the finest structure of its kind in this country. Someone who longed to keep this Castle in her family after she was gone, who left it in her will to her grandson and all his heirs forever.

Perhaps she felt a part of her would always remain here, and she wished to be a part of her descendants' lives.

Perhaps she waits for them.

Or perhaps she just loved this land and her Castle too much to ever leave it.

One of the pictures on the wall leading up the stairs to the guestrooms is of Carrie M. Collins. She is posed with an emotion of contentment on her face, as if she has found her home and wants nothing more—and having discovered that peace, never wishes to leave.

She died in 1926, which of course fits our timeline—there were no prevalent stories of the lady in white before then; but they started and gained enough of a foothold by 1936 to be included in Carmer's book. If it is she, then her spirit came at an opportune time, ripe to latch onto a lingering tale based on fact yet already stretching into something more fantastic.

This was my initial theory, early into researching this tale, and two stories told to me by Margaret Wilson nearly a year later, only strengthened this further. As a young girl staying in the Castle right after Carrie's death, Wilson was afraid to be left alone in that big house—even when her parents were there it was easy to be alone and scared in such a mansion. But there was more—one vivid memory young Wilson has is that of begging her mother not to leave her alone because something in the house terrified her. Margaret's mother took her aside, and very seriously told her not to be afraid, and that the presence she was sensing was only that of Carrie Collins. And since while she was alive Mrs. Collins liked Margaret, it would be no different now, and she had nothing to fear.[1]

The second anecdote relates how Alec Ramage, Margaret's father, had a conversation with Carrie while he drove her to Clifton Springs Spa. Carrie was very ill, and knew her time was running out, and she was doing what she could to alleviate her suffering. Alec told his daughter that Mrs. Collins made him promise to look after Belhurst, and to take good care of it. When he said he would, she replied, "you had better. Because I will be watching."[2]

There are of course, other theories, and the sighting of the woman in white, as mentioned before, is just one of many. A sensitive mind may pick up any number of odd sounds or visions. There may be a man with a cap and sweatshirt just sitting and resting in the corner of your room, or you may feel the tread of little children's feet on you as you sleep, or you may hear a soft voice singing out on the lawn, or during dinner your glass might not be just where you left it. There are all sorts of possible explanations as to what is happening. Maybe it's the land, and as the Senecas warned, there will be trouble if it's not honored properly. Belhurst is in the vicinity of ancient burial grounds, remember—and we're all familiar enough with that cliché.

Or, maybe, as Stephen King often writes, some houses just have something about them, something that retains impressions, feelings, emotions. Images and sounds. There may not be actual ghosts—but only impressions of the departed left behind like footsteps in the snow. Maybe the land is sacred for a reason, and maybe there's some power here that science can't explain.

Then there have been those who have come, heard the stories, and dismissed them all based on the appearance of the Castle, its ivy-covered walls, creaking wooden floors, and general appearance as a typical haunted house. It's all chalked up to a setting capable of evoking illusions of spirits and playing games with our minds.

---

1. Interview with Margaret Wilson, August 2003.
2. Ibid.

There are many more theories, just as there are many more stories here. And I am sure there will be more to be told in the years to come. In the meantime, the Belhurst Castle will stand as it ever has, patiently keeping its mysteries, and inviting investigation.

As for me, on a return overnight visit several months ago, I saw no visions, and slept in complete peace the entire night without the slightest disturbance.

APPENDIX

Unanswered Questions &
Further Research Areas

Unfortunately, my research in some cases led to dead ends. Some areas of investigation were crucial while others would have been 'just nice to know.' The following are some of the open-ended questions that remain, and someday I hope to discover answers for. Of course, if you, the reader find them first, please let me know. There's always room for a second edition of this book...

1. Isabella Robinson (Jane Angus)—what exactly was her relationship to the Covent Garden? How did she find her way to the stage there? Had she performed elsewhere? What happened to her twin brother William?

2. William Henry Hall—what was his wife's name, when was he treasurer of Covent Garden and for how long (definitely 1830, but the duration may have been too small to note, or he may have been an assistant treasurer...)?

3. The Browns (Daniel and James). I have a listing for James Brown as an attorney in Geneva during the 1840's, but apart from that and the fact that on the title transfer they are said to be from New York City, there is nothing on who they were.

4. Harrison Gale Otis bought the place from the Browns in 1852. Hawley refers to him as a 'General', and recalls that he was frequently called away on military missions. What kind of military career did he have? What position did he serve in the Civil War? How did he get his wealth?

5. Carrie Collins is often referred to as a 'direct descendent of Henry Clay'. How exactly is she related? Her father's name was John Young (born 1798, NH) and her mother was Caroline Moore (born 1806, OH). I traced the

Henry Clay lineage down two generations and found neither of these names, and couldn't find either of her parents' parents.

6.   It would be interesting to find out what happened to Rev. Sanborn's 'giant' Indian skeleton that he shipped off to Cambridge for further study.

7.   Lawrence Clark—druggist co-worker (possibly) of Louis Collins in NYC, and resident of Geneva who returned there in 1887. Could he coincidentally and possibly be a descendent of the Rev. Orin Clark who owned the property in the early 1800s?

8.   Hal Harron the 1ˢᵗ (Carrie's son)—what was his story? Who did he marry? Was Hal Jr. his only child? Why did neither of these men wish to stay at the Castle? Did Hal Jr. have any children? Does he have descendants that may still have his grandmother's skeleton, and perhaps more importantly, a diary or some notes on her years at the Belhurst Castle?

9.   Why did Carrie and Samuel divorce? Why was Louis Dell Collins living in Samuel's household from at least 1880—1885? Did he and Carrie have an affair during that time, and consequently they sought out a distant place to live? Or did Carrie visit Geneva first, become enamored of the setting and grew determined to live there at all cost, with or without Samuel?

Bibliography

A History of the Royal Opera House, Covent Garden 1732-1982, Royal Opera House, 1982.

Carmer, Carl, Listen For A Lonesome Drum, New York, Blue Ribbon Books, 1936.

Cleveland, Stafford C., History and Directory of Yates County, Penn Yan, 1873.

Conover, George, History of Ontario County, Feb. 13, 1888, Geneva Historical Society.

Emmons, E. Thayles, The Story of Geneva, The Geneva Daily Times, Geneva, NY, 1931.

The Finger Lakes Times, Geneva NY.

The Geneva Directory, 1911, Geneva Historical Society.

The Geneva Gazette, Geneva NY [microfilm].

The Geneva Advertiser, Geneva NY [microfilm].

The Geneva Daily Times, Geneva NY [microfilm].

Geneva Town Hall, Burial Records (1880-1950).

Hawley, George M.B., Personal Notes, Warren Hunting Smith Library Archives, Geneva, NY.

Hawley, George M.B., Scrapbook & Description of Geneva Homes, Warren Hunting Smith Library Archives, Geneva, NY (1936).

Historical Statistics of the United States, USGPO, 1975. (www.westegg.com/inflation)

Jones, Louis Clark, <u>Things That Go Bump In The Night</u>, New York : Hill and Wang, 1959.

Rochester Democrat & Chronicle, Rochester, NY.

Summary of Findings (Land Title Summary) of Belhurst Castle, Geneva Historical Society, Geneva, NY.

Turner, O. <u>History of the Pioneer Settlement of Phelps' and Gorham's Purchase, and Morris' Reserve.</u> Rochester: Lee, Mann and Company, 1851.

Wyndham, Henry Saxe, <u>The Annals of Covent Garden Theater</u>, London, Chath & Windus, 1906.

0-595-29369-7